The MARITIME MARAUDER *of* REVOLUTIONARY MAINE

The MARITIME MARAUDER of REVOLUTIONARY MAINE

CAPTAIN HENRY MOWAT

HARRY GRATWICK

THE History PRESS

Published by The History Press
Charleston, SC 29403
www.historypress.net

First published 2015

Manufactured in the United States

ISBN 978.1.62619.518.9

Library of Congress Control Number: 2014955493

This book is dedicated to Captain John Flint, a resident of Cushing, Maine, who died in 2013. Without his encouragement and support the book would not have been possible.

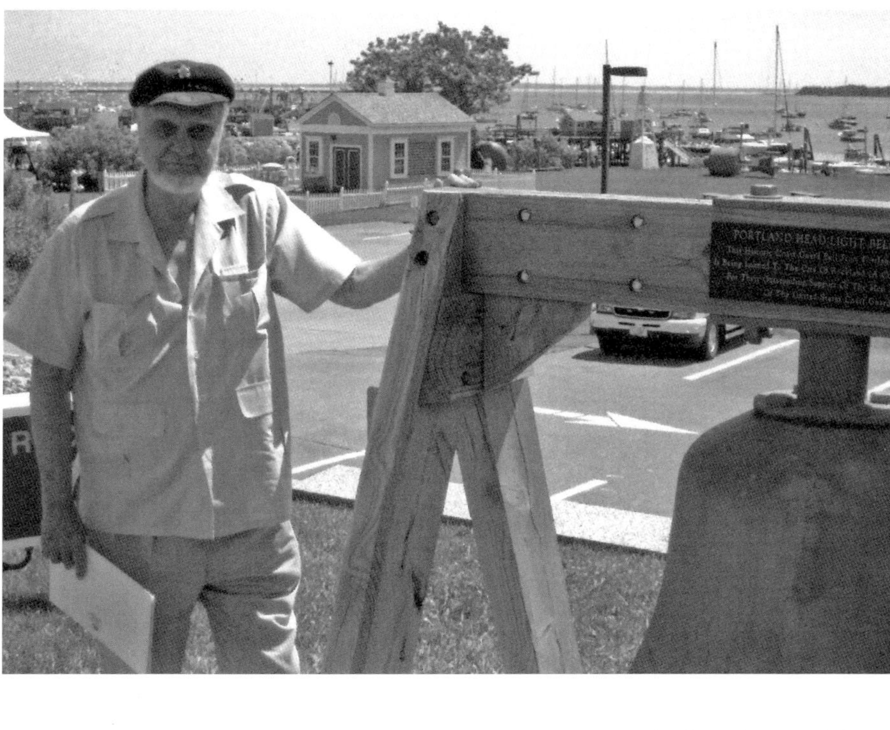

The author is indebted to John Flint for sharing his research on the life of Henry Mowat. *Author's collection.*

The Mowat Controversy

An outrage exceeding in Barbarity & Cruelty every hostile Act practiced among civilized nations.

—George Washington, when informed of the burning of Falmouth Neck (Portland).

Was Henry Mowat a vengeful miscreant, or a duty-bound naval officer operating within a narrow range of choice? Either way, his role in the history of Revolutionary Maine is significant.

—Louis Arthur Norton, professor emeritus, University of Connecticut.

An execrable scoundrel, infamous incendiary and monster of ingratitude.

—Reverend Samuel Dean, pastor, First Parish Church, Portland, Maine.

It is sufficient for us to say that Henry Mowat ruthlessly and needlessly destroyed a thriving and well ordered town peopled with men and women of his own race scattered them abroad exposed to suffering and death form want hardship and exposure.

—James Phinney Baxter, mayor of Portland and Maine historian.

His name lives to be execrated, and his dark deeds are portrayed to teach base men, what indelible infamy shall cleave to their memories.

—William D. Williamson, nineteenth century Maine politician and historian.

No objective historian would attribute ultimate responsibility for the destruction of Hiroshima to the crew of the Enola Gay. Likewise, Lieutenant Mowat as commander of the flotilla had orders, which he carried out.

—William Barry, archivist, Maine Historical Society.

Contents

Foreword

Harry Gratwick's insightful, beautifully rendered portrait of British naval officer Henry Mowat gives us for the first time a clear picture of one of the more important but, until now, dimly understood figures in America's early history. On October 18, 1775, Mowat was the commanding officer of a four-ship squadron that, without provocation, conducted a massive bombardment of Falmouth (now Portland), Maine, wreaking havoc on its citizens, destroying their city and forcing them to flee from their homes just as winter was approaching.

Reaction to what can only be described, even from the perspective of 240 years, as a shocking war crime was instantaneous. The merciless destruction of the most important seaport in the Maine District of Massachusetts spread horror and anger throughout America, uniting the thirteen colonies as never before. Calls for independence multiplied, making the sacrifices necessary to fight the greatest military power of the age much easier to make. More than ever, Americans were determined not to become second-class citizens in an empire dominated by a small elite of landed aristocrats who could inflict such atrocities from three thousand miles away.

On hearing of the extreme reaction to the pitiless treatment of Falmouth, wiser heads in London soon realized that Mowat's raid was counterproductive, and they quickly distanced themselves from him and his superior in Boston, Vice Admiral Samuel Graves, claiming they had gone too far. But, as Harry Gratwick deftly explains, this was not the case. Mowat was carrying out a policy that the hardliners who ruled Britain had been advocating for months, indeed years. A few smart blows, they believed, would frighten provincials into submission. Graves and Mowat were simply following the dictates of their superiors.

Regardless of who was ultimately responsible, however, Graves and Mowat became convenient scapegoats. Mowat suffered the most because he had a long career. No matter how well he performed his duties—and by any measure he performed them well, as Harry Gratwick shows—Mowat's contemporaries were promoted while he languished in the same rank year after year. Understandably, he became bitter. But American patriots, who knew nothing of his difficulties, would have been pleased to learn of his treatment by the very people who were responsible for the orders that got him into trouble. Working up sympathy for the man who had destroyed Falmouth and inflicted so much pain in pursuit of a military strategy that had the exact opposite effect from the one intended was impossible.

George Daughan was the recipient of the 2008 Samuel Eliot Morison Award for Naval Literature for his book If By Sea.

Acknowledgements

Writing a book about an obscure eighteenth-century British sea captain presented a number of challenges, not the least of which was to locate sufficient sources dealing with his career. In addition to John Flint, I would like to thank the following people for their encouragement in helping me research the life of Henry Mowat: Linda Hall at the Williams College Library; Desirée Butterfield-Nagy, archivist and special collections librarian at the Fogler Library, University of Maine–Orono; Gail Judge at Public Archives, Halifax, Nova Scotia; Paige Lilly at the Castine Historical Society; Bill Barry, Sofia Yauloris and Nicholas Noyes at the Maine Historical Society, Portland, Maine; Terry Cole Ranger at Fort Point State Park; and Nina Coffin, graduate assistant at LaSalle University.

In addition, I am grateful to historians George Daughan, Jim Leamon and Charles Bracelen Flood for their suggestions in my pursuit of the often-elusive life of Henry Mowat.

Finally, a salute to my wife, Tita, for her editorial expertise, her love and her cheerful support.

Introduction

Henry Mowat was descended from a family of Scottish seafarers. Legend has it that one of his ancestors was a nobleman who survived the Spanish Armada and settled on the Orkney Islands, which is where Henry was born. This makes a good story, though there is compelling evidence that the founder of the Mowat clan in England was a member of the 1066 Norman Conquest whose descendants later moved to Scotland.

William Barry, archivist at the Maine Historical Society, likens Mowat to C.S. Forester's fictitious British naval hero Horatio Hornblower. Both men were capable and daring Royal Navy officers whose actions were often handicapped by unimaginative, plodding superiors. The chief difference between the two was that, unlike the successful and well-connected Hornblower, Mowat's career was long and mostly undistinguished. As we shall see, it was also highly controversial.

Barry adds, "In the sweep of Maine history probably no man has come in for more personal abuse and less study than the officer who directed the burning of Falmouth-Neck (now Portland)." For two hundred years, Mowat has been vilified in print as "an execrable scoundrel and monster of ingratitude," "the Villain of Falmouth" and "Mad Henry Mowat." In various accounts of the event, he has been described as "the Miscreant of the Maine Coast" and "Maine's arch-villain." After hearing of Mowat's actions, George Washington added, "I know not how to detest him."

Introduction

History has not been kind to Henry Mowat. Although he is best known for the burning of Falmouth in 1775, Mowat's impact on Maine during the American Revolution was not limited to this act. Six months before torching Falmouth, he was charged, erroneously it turns out, with the dismantling of Fort Pownall at the mouth of the Penobscot River. At the time, this angered and alarmed the people living in the area for two reasons. First, they were opposed to the extension of British control along the coast. Secondly, it spread fear that without the fort, the area would be more vulnerable to Indian attack.

Prior to the Revolution, Lieutenant Mowat had led an extensive survey of the Maine coast as well as the Gulf of St. Lawrence in HMS *Canceaux* from 1764 to 1776. The resulting charts were known as the *Atlantic Neptune* and proved to be of benefit to colonial mariners as well as to the British navy. And yet, at the same time he was carrying out the coastal survey, the ever-vigilant Mowat was seizing colonial merchant ships suspected of smuggling and confiscating their cargoes.

Once the Revolution broke out, Mowat's reputation as a seagoing policeman, in addition to his detailed knowledge of the bays and inlets of the coast derived from the *Atlantic Neptune* project, made his name one to be feared by down east sailors.

This was never more evident than in 1779 when Mowat figured prominently in the rout of an American fleet attempting to capture the Loyalist town of Castine, then known as Bagaduce. The event was known as the Penobscot Expedition. Although not as famous as the bombing of Pearl Harbor, naval historians consider the unsuccessful mission to be the worst defeat of an American fleet until 1941, when Japanese planes sank or damaged sixteen warships in the United States Pacific Fleet.

In addition to studying the impact of Henry Mowat on the Province of Maine during the Revolution, a secondary focus of this book will be to examine the question of whether the beleaguered Scottish captain deserved his reputation among Mainers as an "execrable monster." Alternatively, was he simply a duty-bound naval officer operating within a narrow range of limitations? Whichever view one takes, Mowat's role in Maine's history is significant. In either case, he deserves to be called the "the maritime marauder of Revolutionary Maine."

Chapter 1
The Scottish Sailor

It is better to go to jail than to go to sea. At least in jail you are not apt to be drowned.
—*Samuel Johnson*

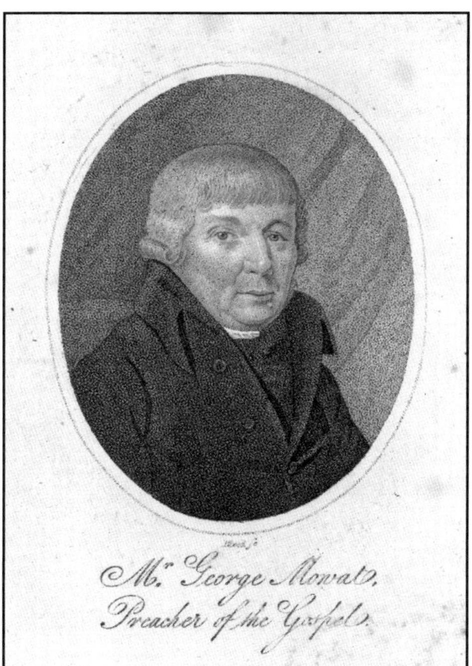

George Mowat was a minister and a cousin of Henry Mowat who lived in New Brunswick, Canada, in the mid-nineteenth century. *Courtesy of the Maine Historical Society.*

As noted, the origins of the Mowat name can be traced back to Normandy stemming from the surname Monhaut or, in Latin, de Monte Alto. In researching the origins of the family, David R. Jack wrote the following description in 1908: "In the hallway of the residence of Mr. George Mowat at Beech Hill near St. Andrews, New Brunswick, hangs a small frame containing the family coat of arms." The crest is an oak tree

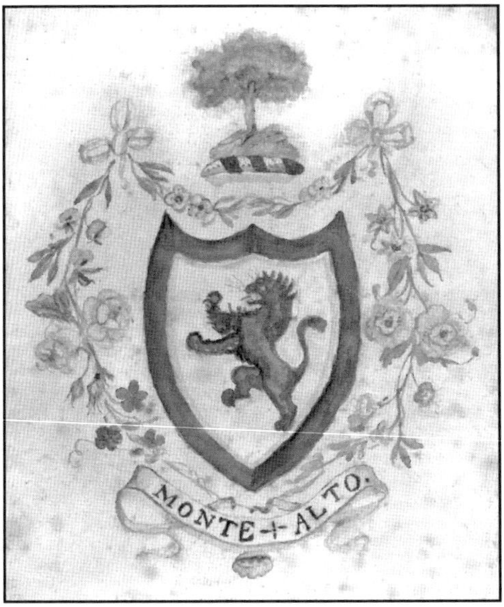

The Mowat family crest. *Courtesy of the Maine Historical Society.*

growing out of a rock. Below is the motto "Monte Alto," meaning on a high mountain. The crest in the Mowat hallway is similar to the one in *Fairbairn's Crests of Great Britain.*

The first member of the Mowat family to arrive in Scotland was Robert de Montealto, who came from Wales in the twelfth century. His family had moved there after an ancestor had accompanied William the Conqueror. Robert de Montealto is believed to have come at the invitation of the Scottish king David I (1124–1153).

The Mowat family's power and prestige increased during the

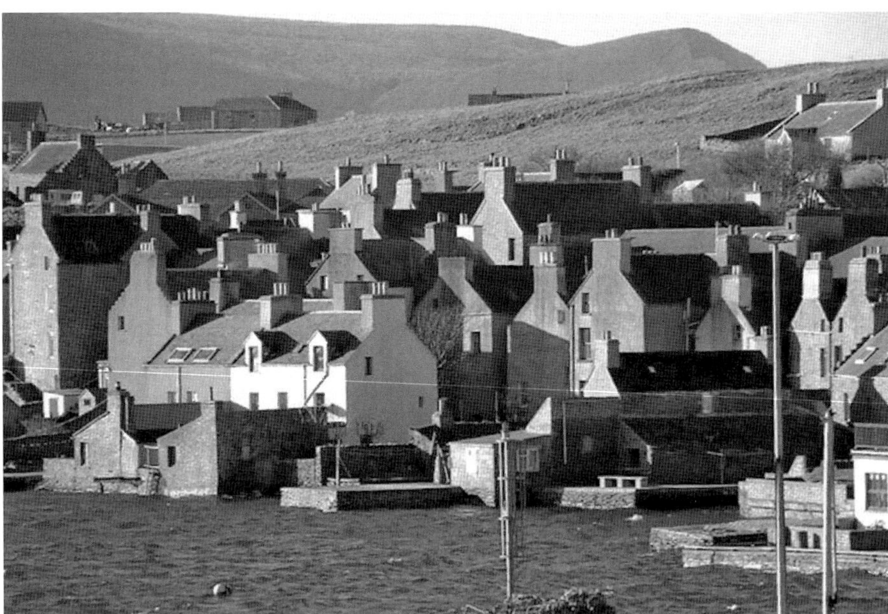

Henry Mowat grew up in the village of Stromness on the Orkney Islands. *Courtesy of Wikipedia.*

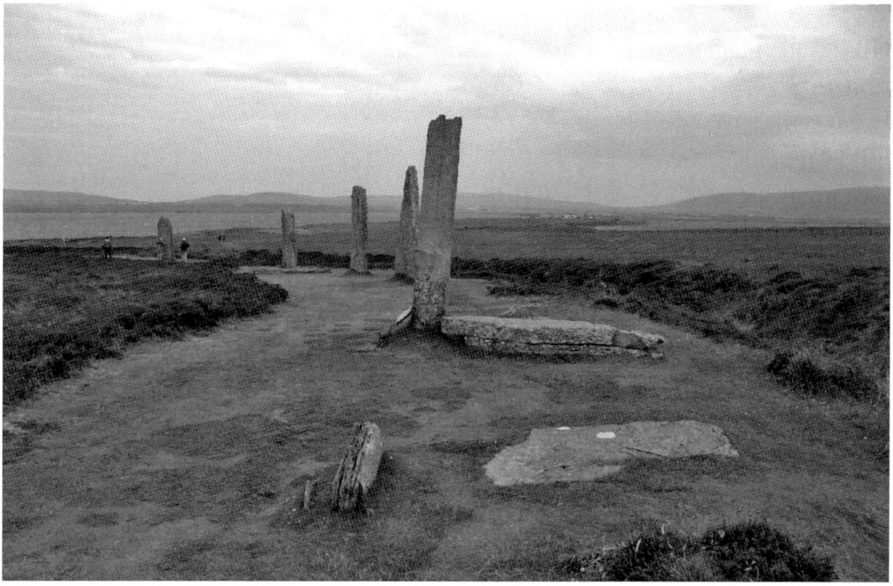

The Neolithic stone circle at Brodgar near Stromness continues to attract tourists. *Courtesy of Wikipedia.*

reign of William the Lion (1165–1214) when William de Montetalto was granted the Lordship of Ferne in Angus. A branch of the family eventually moved on from this area in northeastern Scotland to the Orkney Islands, where Henry Mowat was born in 1734.

In the realm of folklore, there are still a few souls who persist in supporting the idea that the origins of the Mowat family in Scotland were Spanish. Their belief was that the Orkney Mowats were descended from a Spanish nobleman whose ship was wrecked following the defeat of the Armada in 1588. Although a good tale, historically it is apocryphal.

The nearest of the storm-swept Orkney Islands lies twelve miles off the northern coast of Scotland, and it was here that Henry Mowat was born in the village Stromness. The hamlet lies high on a bluff above the great naval anchorage of Scapa Flow. The lands around Stromness have changed little since Henry Mowat's time. The ruins of the bishop's palace still lie across the road from the great red sandstone of St. Magnus Cathedral. Nearby, the massive Neolithic stone circle at Brodgar and the tomb at Maeshowe, erected at the time of the pyramids, still attract tourists.

At one time, the Orkney Islands resounded with the Mowat name, although it is now nearly forgotten. In the cemeteries of Stromness and nearby Kirkwell, Mowat gravestones appear frequently, for the name was among the most illustrious in the island's history. In the Jacobite rising of 1715 by James Francis Edward Stuart, the family backed the wrong side. Unfortunately for his followers, the "Old Pretender" failed in his attempt to regain the British throne.

As a result, the family had lost their lands and titles by the time Henry Mowat was born. His grandfather was incarcerated for debt, and his father spent his much of his life struggling against the load of bonds and obligations. Therefore, the birth of a son to Lieutenant Patrick Mowat of the Royal Navy received little notice. For an Orcadian boy whose ancestors had included a bishop and an admiral, it was an inauspicious beginning.

Young Henry and his three younger brothers grew up hearing tales of Francis Drake and the Spanish Armada. With a father who was an officer in the Royal Navy (he accompanied Captain Cook on his Pacific explorations) and a deceased uncle who had been an admiral, the boys' future was preordained.

As noted, however, there was a problem. Patrick Mowat's side of the family was tainted politically as well as impoverished. Even in the best of times, obtaining a commission in the Royal Navy required a powerful patron willing to post a boy to a midshipman's billet for a substantial sum. Although he would eventually command a ship in the Royal Navy, Patrick Mowat's rank as a lieutenant meant he did not have the clout or finances to open any of these doors, and these were not the best of times.

For Henry, however, there was an alternative. The Royal Navy in the eighteenth century was woefully lacking in competent officers. Thus the navy turned to the professional merchant marine or the maritime "underclass" to sail and maintain the ships of their great fleets. The bulk of these navy men were recruited, or "seized," from the merchant marine. Indeed, fortunate was the Royal Navy captain who had merchant marine officers under his command.

Patrick Mowat's four sons received a better than average education at Stromness schools, where they developed skills in writing, grammar and mathematics. It was in school that Henry would exhibit the stubborn streak that was to last throughout his life. We do not know about his brothers' academic achievements, but Henry was an enterprising student who made an important decision as he neared the end of his formal education. (Little else is known about his brothers except that they also joined the navy and presumably became officers. All three were killed in naval actions in the Caribbean in the 1790s.)

Through his father's limited connections, Henry was able to obtain a berth aboard a local merchant vessel. For more than three years, the young man learned navigation and seamanship under the guidance of an experienced ship's master. Henry showed a flair for leadership and might well have expected promotion to mate and the probability of becoming a ship's master in the merchant marine at an early age. It was here, however, that he demonstrated the stubbornness that would characterize his career. Henry told his father that he would be leaving the merchant marine and intended to become an officer in the Royal Navy.

Armed with an introductory letter from the captain of the merchant ship attesting to his excellent service, as well as one from his father who was now Captain of HMS *Dolphin*, Henry Mowat headed for the great British naval base at Portsmouth. It was here that he hoped to meet Captain Clark Gayton of HMS *Antelope*. With hat in hand, he presented himself to the officer of the deck.

The conversation might have gone something like this. "Sir, I am here to volunteer and I have two letters for Captain Gayton." The officer probably gaped at the respectful young man. (Remember, this was an age when sailors were normally pressed into the navy against their will and here was a youth who actually wanted to volunteer.) Within an hour, Henry Mowat had received the "King's shilling" (a signing bonus) and was enrolled as an able-bodied seaman in the Royal Navy. Thus the enterprising Mowat joined the British Navy in the spring of 1755 at the age of twenty-one.

Here we might pause and reflect on the Samuel Johnson quote cited at the beginning of the chapter: "It is better to go to jail than to sea. At least in jail you are not apt to be drowned." Of course, many men did enlist in the Royal Navy, particularly if the alternative was jail. Those who did so almost immediately regretted their decision. The greatest number of "recruits" was impressed. A more accurate term might be "shanghaied" in that they were snatched from the street or from other merchant ships. The almshouses and courts were also handy resources. A Royal Naval vessel refused no one.

Many recruits were boys, too young to be common seamen, who were relegated to the worst jobs aboard ship. As new crewmembers, their life was brutal, characterized by barbarous discipline. The pay was low, the food miserable and there was no chance to go ashore. Leave was determined solely at the discretion of the captain.

These conditions notwithstanding, young Mowat had no choice but to take this route if he was to follow his dream. Captain Gayton of HMS *Antelope* would determine his immediate future. With his seagoing experience and good education, the new recruit was not just another seaman and the crew soon realized this. Although he was a new hand, Mowat was not subject to the usual harassment from his shipmates, who knew that within a few months, he would become their superior.

It soon became evident that Mowat would be "rated" (a petty officer) and carry the rattan "starter" (a cane or switch) of a master's mate. Indeed, five months later, in November 1755, he was transferred from *Antelope* to HMS *Chesterfield* where he served for the next two years as a master's mate until 1757. Aboard the British battleship of the day, known as a ship of line, the master and his mates were directly subordinate to the first lieutenant, who was the ship's executive officer.

In reality, it was the master who ran the ship, and there was little for which he was not responsible. This ranged from the sailing, navigation and upkeep of the vessel to maintaining the ship's stores and even the writing of the log. Needless to say, the bulk of this work was performed by several of HMS *Chesterfield*'s master's mates, one of whom, for two years, was Henry Mowat.

The multitude of tasks and responsibilities for the master's mates created a practical, hands-on experience for these men. It was a seagoing trade school offering instruction in all the skills expected, but seldom found, among the regularly commissioned "gentleman" officers. It also provided an introduction to the Royal Navy with all of its rules, regulations and paperwork for the proper conduct of a ship and its company. John Flint, a former merchant marine officer, tells us, "It is a sad commentary on the Royal Navy that it rarely reaped the benefits of commissioning these men who were so superbly trained." They didn't fit the image of the "officer class." Henry Mowat, however, would be an exception.

When Mowat was appointed a midshipman in the Royal Navy and transferred to HMS *Chesterfield* in 1755, he had taken the all-important first step into the officer class. Midshipmen, however, were neither fish nor fowl. Most were appointed by senior admiralty figures and entered the service as boys between the ages of twelve and fourteen. Their quarters below decks were dark and dirty, a shadow world above the bilges, lit by tallow candles but supplied with an ample amount of rum.

Midshipmen were the most junior officers, with authority only over the common seaman. They shared their quarters with many others: older midshipmen, master's mates and assorted ship's clerks. Many of these were middle-aged men unlikely ever to become officers. All were at the beck and call of ship's officers and the ship's master. It was a rough and ready existence filled with hazing, beating and bullying, but it was the route the prospective young officer was expected to take.

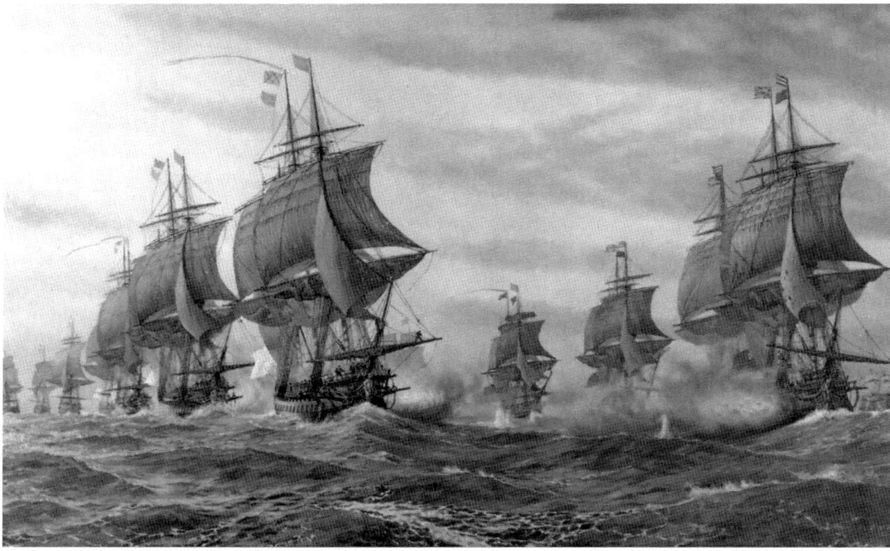

An eighteenth-century naval battle between England and France, similar to the one in which Henry Mowat was involved in 1756. *Courtesy of Wikipedia.*

Henry Mowat entered this world when he went aboard HMS *Antelope*, and it continued when he was transferred to HMS *Chesterfield*. Even with his merchant marine background and his father's reputation, Mowat's advancement was not automatic. He did, however, have several advantages. He was older than most of the youthful midshipmen, he was an experienced mariner and, compared to many of his shipmates, he was an educated man who, according to reports, carried himself with a certain bearing.

With a senior officer acting as their instructor, Henry and other midshipmen would have studied composition as well as learned the routine, customs and traditions of the Royal Navy. As a dogsbody (a drudge) to the ship's officers, Mowat would also have polished his navigation, gunnery, signal and leadership skills. On occasion, he would have been coxswain of the captain's gig (launch), all the while taking verbal abuse from the commissioned officers, who had all undergone the same hell.

We know that Midshipman Mowat saw action aboard HMS *Chesterfield* in May 1756. The forty-four-gun frigate was a member of the British force involved in a major naval engagement with the French during the Seven Years' War. The fleet was under the command of Admiral John Byng and was badly beaten off the island of Minorca in the Mediterranean Sea. Following the defeat, Admiral Byng was relieved of command. He was subsequently court-martialed and found guilty for "failing to do his utmost"

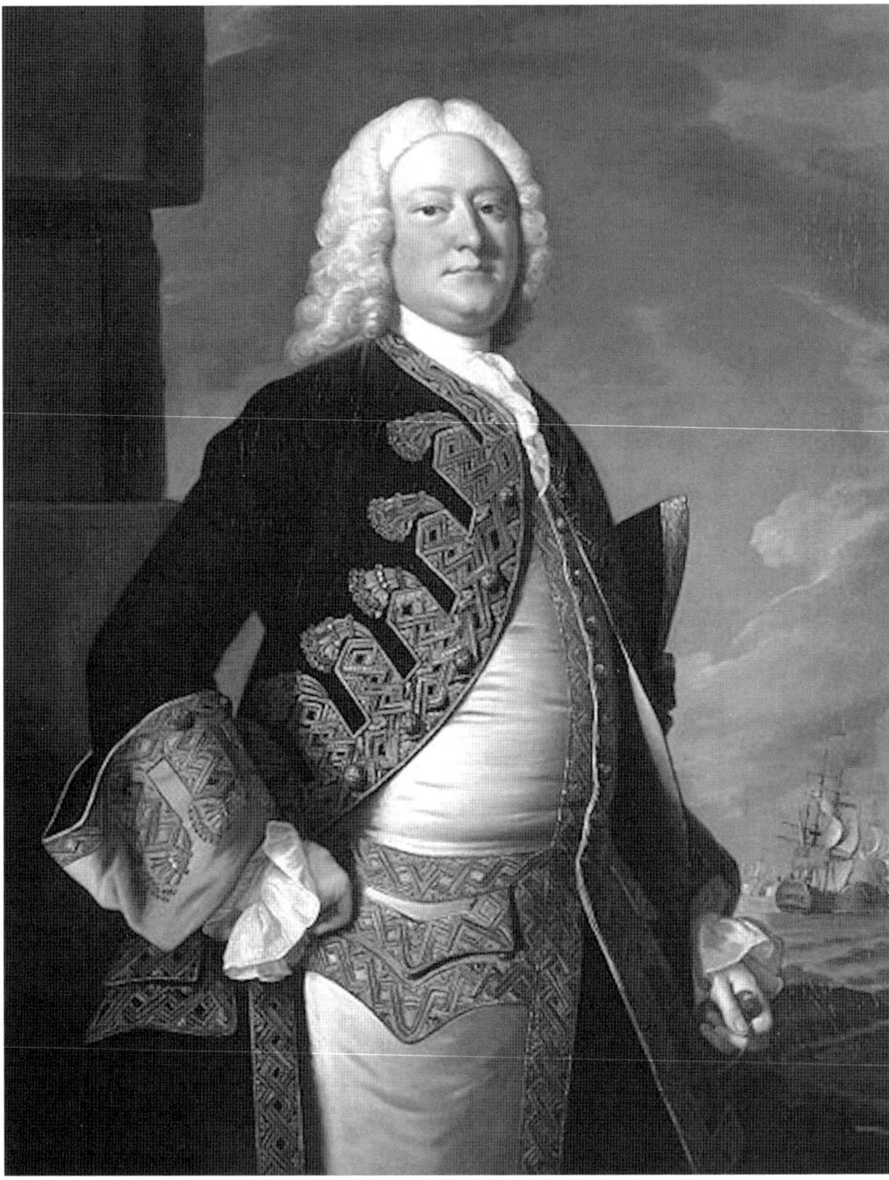

British admiral Byng was executed for having lost the battle of Minorca. *Courtesy of Wikipedia.*

to prevent Minorca falling to the French. Public indignation was so great that the unfortunate Byng was sentenced to death and executed by firing squad in 1757.

Moving to HMS *Ramilles* in August 1757, Henry Mowat would prove his abilities frequently to the officers and captain of that venerable old warship. (It was originally launched in 1664 and rebuilt in 1706.) It was no great surprise, therefore, when he passed his lieutenant's exam on May 9, 1758. The certificate of his "passing" by the admiralty noted:

> *He produceth journals kept by himself in* Chesterfield *and* Ramillies *and certificates from Captains Ogle and Hobbs of his Diligence. He can splice, knot, reef a sail and is qualified to do the duty of an able seaman and midshipman.*

Six months later, on January 21, 1759, Henry Mowat was formally commissioned as a lieutenant in the Royal Navy. Lieutenant Mowat's first assignment as a commissioned officer was aboard the bomb ketch *Baltimore*. He served on the ship, a two-masted vessel armed with mortars, from 1759 to 1760. This was followed by a year's tour on the twenty-four-gun sloop *Aldborough*. His career as a royal naval officer was finally underway.

When the Seven Years' War finally ended in 1763, Great Britain was faced with a huge debt. It was this debt that caused King George III and Parliament to introduce taxation and customs duties on their North American colonies. And twelve years later, this was one of the primary reasons for the outbreak of the American Revolution.

Although England was victorious in the Seven Years' War, the results proved to be ruinous for many officers in the Royal Navy. As the war wound down, Mowat, like many naval officers, was furloughed and put on half-pay. As one officer put it, "The pay was too little to live on but too much to starve on." Henry Mowat would be "on the beach" for almost three years. His next assignment did not come until 1764, but it would be an important step in his career.

Chapter 2

HMS *Canceaux* and the *Atlantic Neptune* Project

The British have over-run more world in three campaigns than the Romans conquered in a century.
—British Prime Minister William Pitt

As Prime Minister Pitt stated in his speech to Parliament at the end of the Seven Years' War, Great Britain's new territories now included lands in North America, India and the Caribbean. By the Treaty of Paris, which ended in 1763, France ceded all of eastern Canada—including Quebec, the present-day maritime provinces and Maine as far as the Kennebec River—to their long-time enemy.

The war brought home to the British military their lack of good maps and charts of North America. More than one battle had been lost by faulty or incomplete geographical information. Since Henry Mowat, as commander of HMS *Canceaux*, would be closely involved in what was to follow, it is important to examine the operation in which he was to play a major role.

The British government asked itself what precisely their country had acquired in North America by the Treaty of Paris? A rough parallel might be drawn with lands the United States purchased from Napoleon in 1803. In that case, the question was what exactly was the extent of the Louisiana Purchase? President Thomas Jefferson's solution was to hire Lewis and Clark

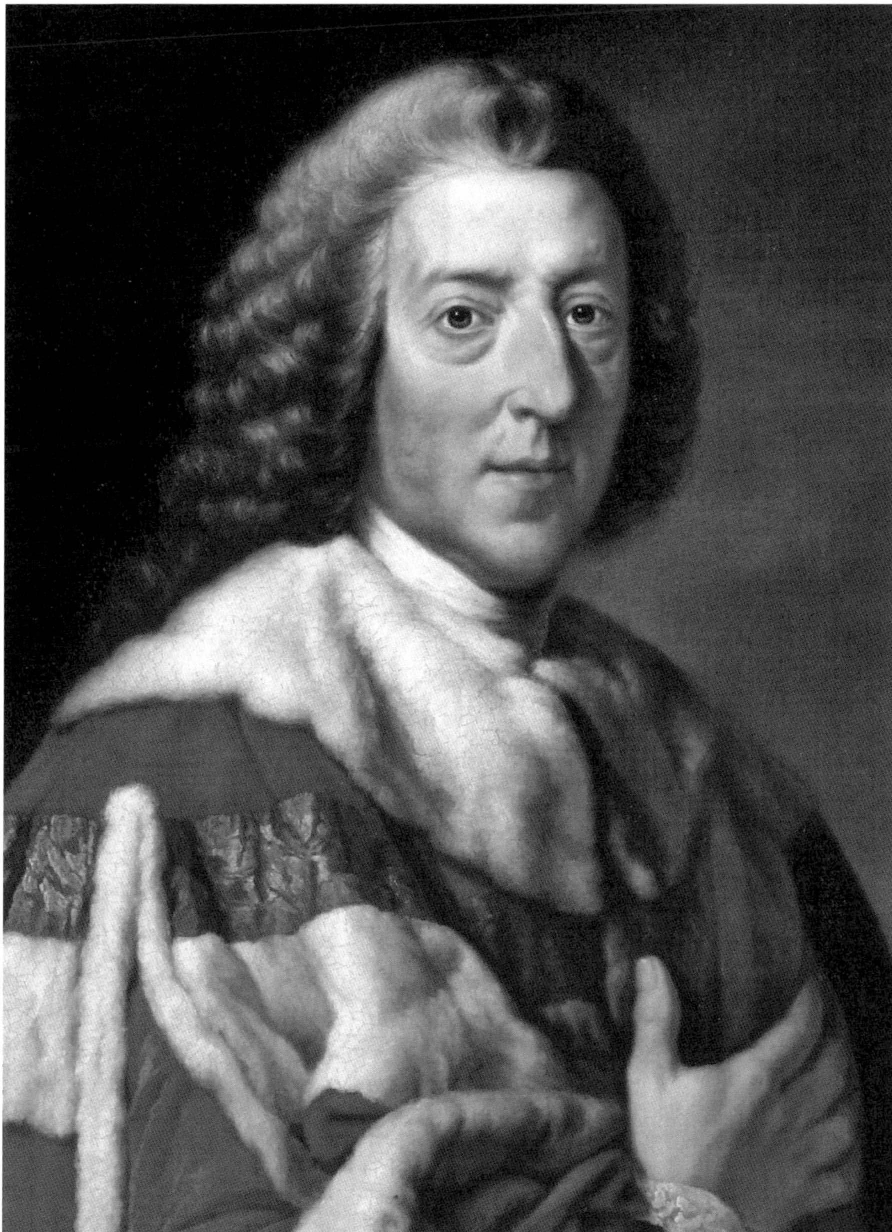

Prime minister William Pitt ordered a survey of the lands Great Britain gained following the Seven Years' War. *Courtesy of Wikipedia.*

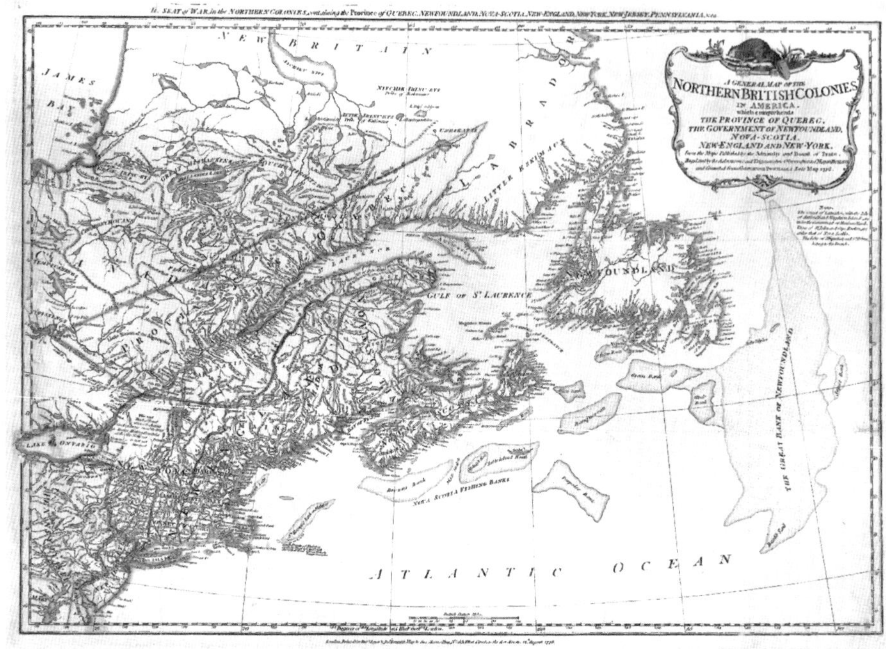

A map of New England and eastern Canada drawn by surveyor Samuel Holland. *Courtesy of the Library and Archives of Canada.*

to explore the extensive lands that ranged from the Mississippi River to the Pacific Ocean.

Perhaps Jefferson was influenced by the actions that had been taken by Great Britain forty years previously in 1763. At that time, the Board of Trade and Plantations and the Lords of the Admiralty ordered a nautical survey of the East Coast of North America and Canada. The result was a monument to the scientific achievement of the European Enlightenment. Published over a ten-year period from 1774 to 1784, *The Atlantic Neptune* was a magnificent four-volume atlas of sea charts and views of the East Coast of North America. The survey alone took twelve years to complete.*

A survey team was put together combining the resources of the board of trade, which made policy decisions for the colonies, and the admiralty.

---

*. Two good accounts of the *Atlantic Neptune* project have recently been published. Andrew J. Wahll transcribed and edited Henry Mowat's logs in his book *Voyage of Canceaux*, which was published in 2003. The second book, *Surveyors of Empire* by Stephen Hornsby, was published in 2011. A complete collection of *Canceaux*'s logs is in the Library of the Maine Historical Society in Portland, Maine.

Each had its own objectives, and not surprisingly, the chain of command was not always clear. As we shall see, thirty-year-old Henry Mowat would occasionally be caught between these two masters.

Two Surveyors

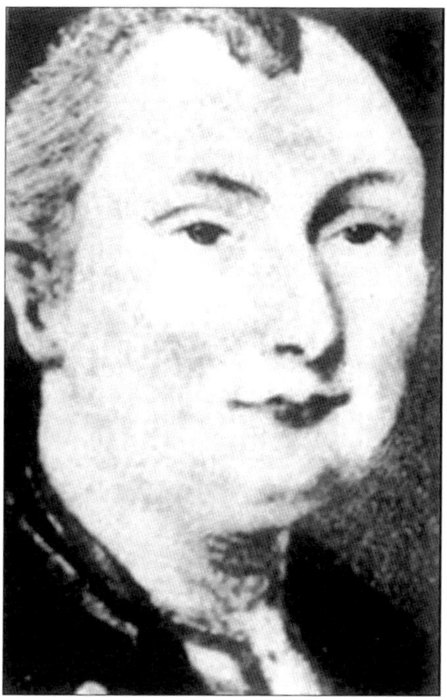

Samuel Holland was a Dutch national who worked as a surveyor for Great Britain on the *Atlantic Neptune* project. *Courtesy of Wikipedia.*

By the end of the Seven Years' War, Samuel Johannes Holland had gained recognition as one of the most capable engineers in the British army in North America. Holland was a Dutch national who had trained as a military engineer in the Netherlands. Faced with a dreary future in the poorly paid Dutch army, Holland joined the British military in 1754 as it prepared to fight the French in the North American theater of the Seven Years' War. The British valued Dutch engineers, and Holland had achieved a reputation as a superb surveyor and mapmaker.

Joseph Frederick Wallet Des Barres began his military career as one of Holland's assistant engineers in the North American campaign. Des Barres was a Protestant who was born in France. He was educated in Switzerland and studied the sciences and mathematics at the University of Basel. Finding his career prospects bleak in Catholic France, Des Barres moved to England and entered Britain's Royal Military Academy, where he focused on military engineering, surveying and map making. Following this, the young cartographer was promoted to lieutenant and posted to North America during the Seven Years' War as an engineer-surveyor in 1756.

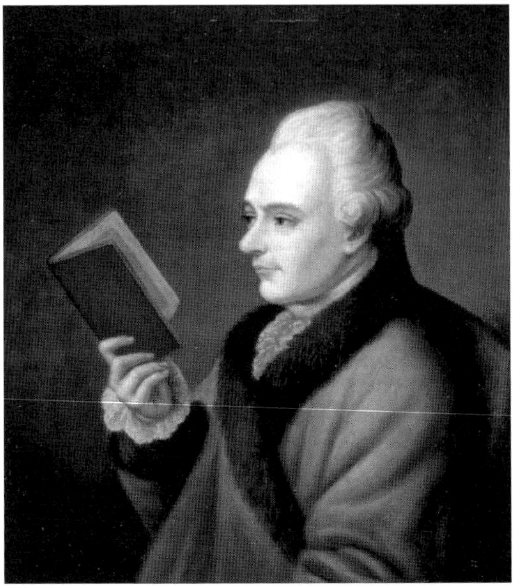

Joseph Wallet Des Barres was a French surveyor who began his career working for Samuel Holland. *Courtesy of the Library and Archives of Canada.*

Holland and Des Barres came to the attention of the British General James Wolfe because of their survey work that had contributed to the capture of Louisburg on Cape Breton Island in 1758. Subsequently, Des Barres would be assigned to Holland's team as the man responsible for mapping the St. Lawrence River. (Another of the surveyors was the Pacific Ocean explorer James Cook.) Using documents captured from the French fortress, Holland, Cook and Des Barres produced detailed charts of the St. Lawrence River.

Their charts were invaluable in enabling the British fleet to move up the St. Lawrence River to the doorstep of the French capital at Quebec. Their land maps were also of crucial importance in General Wolfe's victory at the Plains of Abraham (where he was killed) and the resulting capture of Quebec in 1759. The British victory not only demonstrated the utility of accurate marine surveys, but it also proved Holland's, Cook's and Des Barres's cartography skills to be invaluable assets. As we know, Cook would go on to become renowned for his Pacific voyages and surveys from 1768 to 1779.

Brigadier General Murray recognized Holland's abilities in his report on the *Government of Quebec* to the Board of Trade in 1762. "I can not let slip the opportunity of recommending this gentleman to your Lordship's…He is an industrious brave officer and an intelligent engineer, in which capacity he would be desirous and deservedly merits to be advanced."

Even before the war's end, the board of trade and the admiralty had begun to plan their extensive survey of the eastern seaboard of North America. To do this, they divided the colonies into northern and southern districts with the Potomac River serving as the dividing line. A surveyor general was appointed for each district. William Gerard De Braham, a German emigrant and a longtime resident of Georgia, was selected to survey the southern district.

Samuel Holland was named surveyor general for the northern district. His territories included Prince Edward Island, Cape Breton and the inhabited parts of Canada as far west as Montreal, as well as New England, New York and New Jersey. Joseph Des Barres, Holland's former assistant, was added to the project and directed to "make charts of the coast and harbors of Nova Scotia and Sable Island." (Sable Island is one hundred miles due east of Halifax, Nova Scotia.)

In his book, *Surveyors of Empire*, Stephen Hornsby comments on the differences between the survey techniques of the two men:

> *There was a significant difference between the surveying methods of Holland and Des Barres. Holland was most comfortable surveying on the land—coastlines, rivers, roads, settlements, terrain—and had little aptitude or interest in marine surveying, leaving that to Mowat and the navy. Des Barres had been hired by the Admiralty to conduct a marine survey…These different approaches would be reflected in the charts published in* Atlantic Neptune.

HMS *Canceaux* Underway

The sloop of war *Canceaux* was a converted merchant vessel formerly named *William*. It was purchased by the British Navy at Quebec and brought to the Royal Dockyard at Depford, England, for a refit, which was where Mowat assumed command of the ship. *Canceaux* was eighty-one feet long, carried eight guns and had a crew of forty-five men.

Although he held the rank of lieutenant, Henry Mowat was promised promotion to the rank of "master and commander." Unfortunately, this proved to be an elusive post for the Scotsman.*

In the preface to his book *Voyage of the Canceaux*, Andrew Wahll wryly comments, "Without patronage, exemplary record, or good fortune in surviving combat that killed his superiors, gaining a captaincy would be difficult. Mowat would remain a lieutenant for a long time."

*. In the eighteenth century British navy, a lieutenant or a commander in command of a vessel was called by courtesy "captain" but kept his rank until made a post captain. Admiralty records show that Mowat was finally promoted to the rank of commander on June 2, 1776, and to captain on October 26, 1782. There is a family story that Captain Mowat was promoted to rear admiral in 1798 but died before he could return home.

Henry Mowat's "man Friday" was William Hogg, a midshipman who was also the sailing master. As noted in the first chapter, the ship's master was in charge of maintaining the ship, working the sails, managing the survey work and overseeing the ship's logs.

In his book, Andrew Wahll explains that *Canceaux* was mainly a supply depot, a "mother ship" that provided all manner of goods for the smaller, shallow draft vessels that explored the rivers, bays and offshore islands of the East Coast. A log entry for July 10, 1770, reads: "Supplied *Jupiter* with rope of all sizes, some canvas, twine and other carpenter's stores for use in the survey." These survey boats worked from early spring until well into the fall when "freeze-ups" began.

As we shall see, *Canceaux* was an extremely busy ship. In the evenings and in bad weather, it was a workplace where drafting and the compilation of information from the survey parties were recorded. During the winter months, the ship wintered in a convenient Canadian or New England port. Over a twelve-year period, it only returned to England once for an overhaul, which was during the winter of 1770–71.

At least eight smaller vessels used for surveying were attached to *Canceaux*. Cutters and pinnaces were ships' boats that were hoisted in and out by tackle from the yards. Shallops were somewhat larger and were generally towed. Surveyor General Holland also purchased two schooners, which gave him a base from which to operate when Mowat was off chasing smugglers in *Canceaux*.

For twelve summers, and more than a few winters, the surveyors on these vessels mapped the shorelines of North America. Their assignment was to make rough charts of the coastal waters and nearby land features as they appeared from the water. In addition to exploring rivers and islands, their work included mapping sandbars, locating ledges and shipwrecks, taking bottom soundings and discovering the direction of ocean currents. It was a huge undertaking.

When the northern part of the *Atlantic Neptune* project was completed in 1776, the men associated with the undertaking had surveyed a total of 4,500 miles. This included exploring the St. Lawrence River as far as present-day Montreal, as well as the Canadian and New England coastlines. If we combine the northern and southern districts, the overall survey covered 15,000 miles. Andrew Wahll calls the resulting *Atlantic Neptune* "one of the most important and magnificent coastal marine atlases ever produced."

In the preface to *Canceaux*'s logs, Wahll reminds us that Des Barres, Holland and Mowat were not the only contributors to the survey project. Wahll pays tribute to twenty-five other men. The list includes the captains and surveyors of the eight smaller craft that probed the innumerable estuaries and bays of New England and Canada from 1764 to 1776.

Both Mowat and sailing master William Hogg contributed to the log of *Canceaux*, so we have more than one voice describing the expedition. It would also be incorrect to assume that Henry Mowat was always on board *Canceaux* to direct the project. From the logs, it is clear that he was very active in day-to-day survey operations. There are frequent references to Mowat's activities, presumably written by Hogg. "Captain Mowat went away in the pinnace sounding with seven days provisions." A few days later, "Captain Mowat returned from sounding," October 1, 1766.

The long-range consequences of Mowat's day-to-day involvement with the survey were significant for several reasons. For example, during the American Revolution, the mere mention of his name struck fear in the hearts of Maine mariners because of his extensive and detailed knowledge of the Maine coast. When combined with his aggressive behavior toward smugglers, it is hardly a surprise that he was regarded as "the maritime marauder," before the Revolution began.

It is a tribute to the nautical abilities of Henry Mowat as captain of *Canceaux* that, aside from an occasional grounding in the fog, the ship remained afloat and intact for twelve years, thus enabling the survey teams to carry out their explorations. By 1776, Joseph Des Barres had returned to England and had begun to publish *Atlantic Neptune*. Henry Mowat's career, however, would stagnate. He remained at sea, mostly off the coast of New England, for the rest of his life, increasingly resentful of how he was denied promotion by the admiralty.

Mowat's logs provide us with a valuable insight into the workings of a British warship in the latter part of the eighteenth century. Not surprisingly, most of the references were weather information: "hard squalls with thunder, lightning and rain," and the direction of the wind. Frequent entries also include maintenance of the ship, supplies taken on board and other variations in the ship's routine including discipline meted out, the comings and goings of other ships and the activities of the surveyors.

One of the frequent duties of a ship's commander was to read the thirty-six Articles of War to the assembled ship's company. The first of these entries occurred on June 1, 1764, as *Canceaux* was about to cross the Atlantic. Henry Mowat read the Articles of War at least once a month, usually on Sundays following religious services. It was intended as a reminder to the ship's company as to what was expected of them. It should be noted that of the thirty-six articles, eighteen were punishable by death.

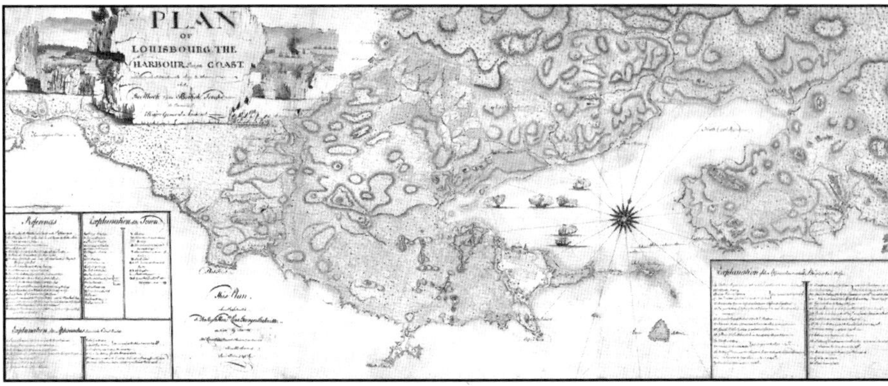

A map of Louisburg drawn by Samuel Holland for the *Atlantic Neptune* project. *Courtesy of the Library and Archives of Canada.*

Life aboard a British man of war was harsh, and Mowat was no different from other captains in applying the lash when necessary. Most punishments were for drunkenness, disobedience, dereliction of duty or "mutinous expression." Over a twelve-year period, Mowat recorded thirty-seven floggings as well as one execution and five accidental deaths.

Some examples: on July 1, 1769, seaman Bolat Watts received thirty lashes, a particularly severe penalty, for drunkenness, neglect of duty and "mutinous expression" (we can only imagine what that meant). Most references to punishment were for twelve lashes, which is what George Davis received for "drunkenness and mutinous expression" on September 1, 1772.

Canceaux passed Land's End, the western tip of Great Britain, on June 11, 1764, and four weeks later the vessel arrived at the citadel of Louisburg on Cape Breton Island. From there the survey ship sailed to Quebec, where it arrived on August 12. Here another problem emerged: desertion. Runaways were always a concern when a royal naval vessel was in port, and *Canceaux* was no exception.

Mowat mentions five men by name who "ran away with a boat," on August 24, 1764. The boat was later found on the Isle of Orleans, five miles from Quebec City, but there is no mention of the men being caught. During the twelve-year cruise, the log lists twenty-five men who deserted from the ship. It is interesting that, over time, the number of runaways declined, which might suggest that most of the malcontents had left the ship or conditions on board improved.

There is no doubt that food was one of the main reasons for joining the British Navy. To have meat four days a week was not a privilege enjoyed by a large part of the English population in the eighteenth century. Normally, sailors had a hot meal every day, which often consisted of beef or pork, beer, bread and cheese and sometimes vegetables and fruit. As long as *Canceaux* was close to land, it received supplies frequently, and Captain Mowat kept a careful record of provisions brought on board. Before a long voyage, the meat was salted, pickled and packed in casks.

The job of keeping his ship stocked with food was vitally important to Captain Mowat. Andrew Wahll writes in his preface to the *Canceaux* logs, "Few things were nearer to the sailor's heart than his stomach." As a result, Mowat went to great lengths and considerable expense to provide his ship with fresh vegetables and fresh meat whenever possible. The job of *Canceaux*'s quartermaster, or supply officer, was a critical one. It was one of the many tasks overseen by sailing master William Hogg.

Log entries pertaining to provisions give us an idea of the massive quantities of food involved in feeding even a small ship. Before *Canceaux* crossed the Atlantic Ocean in May 1764, 570 pounds of fresh beef were loaded aboard for the approximately forty-five crewmen. Before leaving Nova Scotia for its summer cruise in 1767, *Canceaux* took on board 4,000 pounds of oatmeal, 750 gallons of beer, 1,550 pounds of rice and 2,000 pounds of cheese, and this was just a small portion of the food the ship carried that summer.

During the course of the expedition, there were regular references to specific amounts of food the ship received and consumed: "Fresh beef received on board" or "opened a firken [wooden box] of butter" or "received on board a cask of beer" or "opened cask of beef, contents fifty six pieces short" or "opened a cask of pork and found thirteen pieces deficient." The longer *Canceaux* was at sea, the more likely it was a cask would be opened and the contents found to be spoiled. One time, Mowat indignantly wrote, "Returned a hogshead of beer to HMS *Kingfisher*, not fit to drink."

With a crew of forty-five men and another thirty-five in the eight smaller survey vessels, it is surprising that fatal accidents did not happen more often. Over a twelve-year period, Mowat reports only a few deaths. Not surprisingly, most were on the survey expeditions. The circumstances of each death vary and show the perils of eighteenth-century life at sea.

> *December 17, 1765: Frederick Bemand, deputy surveyor to Surveyor Holland, fell through the ice and drowned.*

> *April 7, 1768: Seaman Lawrence May fell from a yardarm above the deck between the ship and the wharf and was drowned.*
>
> *October 13, 1770:* Canceaux *returned to England for repairs, saluted Admiral Grasy with thirteen guns. In loading the gun one seaman was shott* [sic] *fell overboard and was drowned.*
>
> *August 25, 1774: Sloop* Jupiter *(one of the survey boats) was lost to the westward of Cape Cod with all provisions and stores and some men* [the exact number was not stated] *drowned.*

There are frequent references to repairs that were made to *Canceaux* and the eight shallow-draft survey vessels that were used to chart the coastal waters. Any time the weather was good, the ship's carpenters were at work scraping and painting the hull and repairing rigging. Andrew Wahll tells us in his *Canceaux* notes that, in 1761, the British navy began to use thin sheets of copper nailed to the bottom to protect the wooden hulls from fouling.

Although *Canceaux* was sheathed with copper, after long periods of immersion in saltwater, the ship's bottom's needed cleaning. This was called "breaming," which was when shells and seaweed that had gathered on the ship's hull were removed and burned. To do this, *Canceaux* was brought to a shallow area near the shore and anchored. When the tide went out, the ship would come to rest in the mud with its hull exposed. A log entry on September 14, 1765, describes the process: "Heeled ship to port & scrubbed the bottom with razen [sic] tallow & brimstone, heeled to starboard and & scrubbed the same way."

Henry Mowat was a conscientious captain who realized how important it was to keep his crew occupied. Those men not assigned to surveying parties or working on the ship were sent ashore to gather wood for which there was a frequent demand. There are constant references to "people employed wooding."

Maintenance of the ship was ongoing; indeed it was essential, which meant that in all but the worst weather crewmen were busy. A log entry on September 5, 1767, reads, "Employed hands scraping the ships sides, masts and setting the rigging fore and aft." Another critical job was the caulking of the seams, which were constantly opening up. This needed to be done throughout the ship: the hull, the deck, the galley and between decks. The longer the cruise continued, the more frequent the need for caulking. Despite constant maintenance and a refit in England in 1770, after twelve years, *Canceaux* was literally coming apart. It was finally reported to be "unfit to keep at sea" on January 5, 1776. But we are getting ahead of ourselves.

Canceaux was moored off of Kittery on the Piscataqua River, where it received stores and underwent needed repairs in May 1773. Following this, the ship spent most of the summer venturing down east, charting the coast as far as Mount Desert Rock. A letter from Samuel Holland reported that the Maine coast consisted of "a multitude of islands, harbors, bays and inlets in which no parts of America can equal in numbers in such a small extent."

In addition to Holland, *Canceaux* had on board New Hampshire governor Wentworth, who was also surveyor of the King's Woods. At the end of the summer, Henry Mowat received a compliment in the form of a letter that Wentworth sent to the treasury office in London:

> *The ready and most useful aid I have received from Mr. Mowat, in accommodating me with passages to these places, and his unwearied assiduity at all times in assisting me, by every means in his power to carry the laws for preserving pine into execution, but for this gentleman's good disposition and zeal, must have been utterly impossible for me to have so well accomplished.*

From log entries we can follow *Canceaux*'s route across Penobscot Bay as Mowat makes reference to passing, and presumably exploring, the waters around Monhegan Island, Matinicus Rock, Seal Island, Isle au Haut, Cranberry Island and Mount Desert.

At one point, the log noted that *Canceaux* anchored in Cranberry Island Harbor, south of Mount Desert, in a "thick fog" on June 16, 1773, which certainly fits the weather profile of the Maine coast in early summer. Throughout the expedition there are also entries that mention soundings taken in the various island harbors where *Canceaux* anchored. Mowat's log notes suggest that he was becoming familiar with the Penobscot Bay area. As previously noted, this knowledge would serve him well six years later when he was defending Bagaduce (Castine) at the north end of the bay against an advancing American fleet in 1779.

Special Events

Throughout *Canceaux*'s twelve-year odyssey, occasional entries appeared in the log referring to fifteen- or twenty-one-gun salutes ordered by Captain Mowat to mark important dates on the English calendar. Presumably this was intended to remind the crew of the specific event as well as to relieve the tedium of the endless voyage. There were three such "days" during the year that Mowat noted in the log, although there is no indication they were holidays in any other way for the crew.

Guy Fawkes Day celebrated the failed Gunpowder Plot by Roman Catholics, which was discovered on November 5, 1605. It was observed with a salute that varied from thirteen to fifteen guns. (Perhaps the number of cannons fired depended on the amount of gunpowder the ship had available.) This was an entry that was noted most years, though not annually.

Mowat also ordered a twenty-one-gun salute on May 30 to commemorate the Restoration of King Charles II in 1660 following the Interregnum of Oliver Cromwell. There is no record of this occurring every year, but in the latter stages of the voyage, in the 1770s, it became a regular entry. One might speculate that the captain was trying to impress the frequently fractious New England colonists of the importance of the Crown in their lives. For example, while moored in Boston Harbor on May 30, 1774, Mowat's log reads: "Light airs and variable, fired thirteen guns [were they again low on powder?], it being the Restoration of King Charles II."

Five days later, on June 4, 1774, *Canceaux* was still moored in Boston Harbor when Mowat ordered twenty-one-guns fired to commemorate King George III's birthday. He had begun to do this in 1766, two years after the voyage started and five years after the king was crowned. Most years the salutes went off without incident, though occasionally there was an explosion when the previous charge in a cannon barrel was not completely sponged out.

An accident occurred when *Canceaux* was moored at the mouth of the Piscataqua River between Kittery and Portsmouth, New Hampshire, in 1775. One of the celebratory cannons went off prematurely, "carrying away the boatswain's hand." To avoid infection, the surgeon's mate decided to amputate the poor fellow's arm below his shoulder. The stump was then cauterized with a hot steel rod and covered with tar. Somehow the boatswain, drugged with laudanum and rum, survived the resulting shock.

HMS *Canceaux* and the *Atlantic Neptune* Project

The Winter Months

Fresh gales with rain and sleet and snow.
—Canceaux*'s log*

For the first six years of the expedition, *Canceaux* wintered at various British Canadian ports. As long as the weather held, survey teams explored the St. Lawrence River to Quebec and Montreal, as well as the Gulf of St. Lawrence, Cape Breton Island and Nova Scotia.

To give the reader an idea of the frigid weather, records indicate that many men in the British North American Squadron died of frostbite when the sea was frozen for sixty miles off Cape Breton Island in 1760. Men got chilblains from the cold since there was no heat except on the mess desk. Mowat describes, "snow and hard frost AM, fresh gales with snow. Punished John Clark with thirteen lashes for drunkenness and mutinous words," December 5,1765.

Canceaux often spent the winter in the relatively protected, but frequently icebound, harbor below the fortress of Louisburg on Cape Breton Island. It is hard to imagine the conditions of life on shipboard in frigid weather

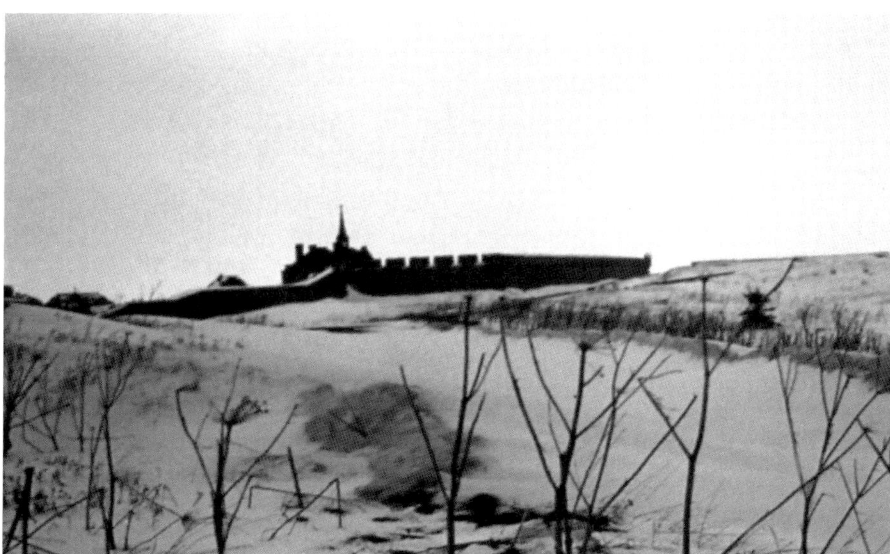

The citadel of Louisburg was a bleak place in the winter. *Author's collection.*

that Mowat had to deal with, and it is not surprising that tempers flared frequently among the crew. The sailors were constantly being soaked by salt water, and with no opportunity to dry their clothes, everyone lived in a state of perpetual dampness.

Of the several winters that *Canceaux* spent at Louisburg, the season from December 1768 to March 1769 was a particularly bad one. It was obviously bitterly cold as the log makes frequent references to "hard frost" and "constant problems with ice": "The Bay all frozen over, crew walked ashore on the ice…great quantities of drift ice about the ship…People employed in cleaning ice off the ship." At one point, Mowat writes, "The anchor and cable were lost overboard." Crewmen were constantly sent aloft to clear ice from the frozen rigging and the sails, which meant exposing their hands to biting temperatures.

St. Patrick's Hole is a sheltered anchorage at the mouth of the St. Patrick River near Quebec, where *Canceaux* stayed from November 1769 to the spring of 1770. Mowat writes that the ship was icebound until late April 1770 and that George Davis was given "twelve lashes for neglect of duty and going ashore without leave," on April 25, 1770. It is remarkable that more men did not go AWOL during the course of the endless winter.

During the more temperate winters, *Canceaux* sailed from one port to another during the cold weather. The harbors it stopped at most frequently were Halifax, Boston and the Piscataqua River, which separates Portsmouth and Kittery. Surveys were attempted, but often the cold weather made it impossible as the log noted on February 10, 1769: "These twenty four hours very severe frost. No possibility of marking. Captain Holland returned." The weather took its toll on the crew as well. The next day, Mowat wrote, "Departed this life of the sea Tom Colevard, seaman."

After eight years of wintering in icebound North American harbors, *Canceaux* was in desperate need of repairs. Indeed, Captain Mowat was alarmed at the deteriorating condition of his ship. Finally, he was ordered to bring the vessel to England for a long overdue refit during the winter of 1770–71. The ship crossed the Atlantic in four weeks carrying on board a contingent of thirty-seven "invalided soldiers" from the Halifax hospital. *Canceaux* dropped anchor at the naval base at Spithead, on the south coast of England on October 12, 1770.

The log reports that two days later, "The invalided soldiers were sent on," (presumably to hospitals on shore) and temporary repairs were made on *Canceaux*'s upper works (masts and rigging). The crew must have groaned at the prospect of the task that lay ahead, although their spirits were lifted when 414 hogsheads of beer arrived on board on October 19.

Orders flew back and forth between Mowat at Spithead and the admiralty in London, and a month later, *Canceaux* weighed anchor and headed up the coast to the Thames River estuary. There a pilot came on board and guided the vessel up the river to the town of Woolrich, just south of London, for a major overhaul.

At the Woolrich naval dockyard known as Gallions Reach, the ship was "unrigged," and the crew was employed in "removing the guns and stores." A number of crewmen were sent to the hospital, others were temporarily transferred to nearby ships and some were kept on board to work on the ship.

There is a gap in *Canceaux*'s log from January 2, 1771, to May 17, 1771, while the ship underwent an overhaul at the Gallions Reach boatyard. By the end of the spring, the ship was repaired and guns were hoisted on board. Mowat was now faced with a problem common to most Royal Navy captains. Because it lacked a full complement of sailors, his ship was unable to join a fleet preparing to sail to North America. Mowat reported in the log: "Not having received the seamen in lieu of those run [deserted] could not weigh at the same time. Hove short lying waiting for the men." This was written on June 12, 1771.

While supplies continued to be brought on board, Captain Mowat proceeded to gather a crew. This consisted mostly of men drafted from other ships. "Fifteen seamen received from *Resolution*…Received seven from *Terrible*." Clearly not all of the sailors were eager to resume the voyage. A log entry on June 6 notes, "Found six men run from the ship that had got ashore in some boat." Finally, on June 17, he noted, "Got thirty men from *Glory* to assist us in getting under sail." It is not stated whether the sailors were returned to *Glory* or stayed on board *Canceaux*.

By mid-June 1771, the survey vessel had finally impressed a full complement of men and it set sail down the channel, stopping briefly at the naval base at Spithead. After a six-month's hiatus, the second half of *Canceaux*'s twelve-year cruise was underway.

MOWAT AND HOLLAND

It took some time for Henry Mowat and Samuel Holland to develop a good relationship. As stated at the beginning of this chapter, Captain Mowat served two masters. In the first year of the survey project, Mowat and Holland had trouble working together when *Canceaux*'s captain refused Surveyor General Holland's request to use the small boats for his crew to do coastal surveying. Mowat's view was that as the ship's captain, he was in charge of the overall survey. Instead of objecting, Holland wisely passed the problem along to the board of trade and the admiralty in London. The reply came a month later to Mowat in the form of a reprimand.

> *The service* [Holland] *is employed upon is of too great importance to be neglected on any account whatsoever…I take occasion to recommend to you in the strongest terms to maintain perfect harmony with Captain Holland, to look upon yourself as a joint labourer with him and to suffer no such distinction as ships duty and surveyor's duty to exist, but…to pursue a cause which is so much the object of his Majesty's attention and care.*

Henry Mowat accepted the rebuke, and henceforth Holland apparently received his full cooperation. Two years later, in 1767, hearing that the captains of armed vessels were to be rotated, Holland wrote the admiralty asking that the order not apply to Mowat. "Notwithstanding some misunderstandings between me and the former I should still be glad to keep him as those matters have been settled and I may have the same disagreeable steps to undergo with his successor." The admiralty accepted Holland's request and Mowat remained in command.

Once the two men reached an understanding, there were constant references in the log to their collaborative efforts. "Captain Holland & his party went out on a survey as did Captain Mowat with the pinnace." Nevertheless, Mowat must have quietly groaned when he saw the endless amounts of equipment Holland kept bringing on board. "Crew employed landing the Surveyor General's baggage," appears frequently.

Mowat was also irritated by the pieces of equipment that were constantly being lost from the survey boats. Although no protests appear in the log, he made extensive lists of what had to be replaced. "Mr. Wright deputy surveyor lost out of his boat during ye summer survey 2 hand leads and 2 lines, 3 oars, boat hook, 2 deep sea lines 1 lead and the boat's mizon [sic]." And then there was the zealous Holland's persistence to survey in spite of bad winter weather. "These 24 hours very severe frost, no possibility of marking, Captain Holland returned."

Finally, there was the ongoing conflict of interest between the board of trade's directive that Mowat give Captain Holland his full cooperation and the instructions from his naval superiors, the admiralty, that he enforce British laws on trade and navigation. Stephen Hornsby notes, "Chains of command were becoming entangled and became ever more so as demands on the navy increased."

The Sugar Act, in particular, posed a problem. The act's purpose was to stop smugglers from bringing cheap molasses from the French West Indies to North American rum distillers. One of the provisions of the act, passed in 1764, prohibited trade between the French islands in the Caribbean and North American ports. Following the Seven Years' War, the size of the British navy had been considerably reduced, putting considerable pressure on those vessels that remained to enforce the law. Since a portion of the proceeds from the sale of a captured vessel went to the captain and his crew, Henry Mowat and the *Canceaux* sailors had a significant incentive to catch vessels engaged in the illegal trade. The result was that Mowat frequently took time off from surveying to search for smugglers.

Canceaux's log is filled with reports of vessels that were "seized." Presumably many were carrying an illegal cargo. In each of these cases, Mowat would have profited from the sale of the captured vessel. It therefore should not be a surprise that he came to be regarded as a scourge to colonial mariners. A sampling of the numerous seizures as recorded in *Canceaux*'s log follows.

> *February 27,1766: At 4 PM Captain Mowat returned with an agreement that he had made seizure of the sloop* George *belonging to Quebec with wine and brandy from St. Peters.*
>
> *October 22, 1767: Brought too* [stopped] *a brig which proved to be* Charming Peggy *belonging to London, last from Guernsey loaded with* [cargo not stated]. *Sent an officer on board & sized* [sic] *her wealth.*
>
> *August 17, 1769: Weighted* [anchor] *and came to sail at 5. Fired a gun and brought too a brig from Falmouth bound to Quebec with wine.*
>
> *October 11, 1769: Fired a gun and brought too a sloop from Boston to Quebec with rum and provisions.*

> *July 18, 1770: Saw a sloop in NW quarter fired two guns & brought too a sloop & schooner from New York bound to Quebec.*

Friday and Saturday, October 5 and 6, 1770, was a particularly active end of the week for *Canceaux*:

> *Saw a ship in the E quarter, fired a gun & brought too, two vessels from N. Carolina bound to Glasgow* [and the next day] *Saw two sails in the E quarter and one in the southern quarter, fired four guns & brought too a ship from Virginia bound to Spain.*

Surveyor General Holland was not pleased with Mowat's role as a seagoing sheriff, and he wrote to the Earl of Hillsborough, who was president of the board of trade. "The naval part is much behind the land part of the survey as the *Canceaux* can not compatibly attend the two businesses of sounding and watching for smugglers."

The smuggling continued, however, and in 1770, Mowat received an ambiguous letter from Rear Admiral Montagu: "To seize all vessels employed in illicit trade, but on no account to deviate from the service of surveying." In spite of the confusing orders, Holland and Mowat continued to work reasonably well together for the next several years. Interestingly, there were fewer references in the log to "seizures" after Mowat received Montagu's letter.

Holland's former assistant surveyor, Joseph Des Barres, was on a different survey ship much of the time and appears infrequently in *Canceaux*'s log. As noted, Des Barres's primary responsibility was surveying Nova Scotia and Sable Island. At one point, an exasperated Des Barres wrote of his assignment:

> *Because of the irregularity of the shoreline, the work was often exceedingly tortuous. There is scarcely any known shore so much intersected with Bays, Harbors and Creeks as this is, and the Offing* [off shore] *of it is so full of Islands, Rocks and Shoals as are almost innumerable.*

Although Des Barres's survey assignment was not as extensive as Holland's, if anything, it was more hazardous. Nor did Des Barres have the luxury of a permanent supply ship like *Canceaux*. He was finally assigned the schooner *Diligent* in 1770, which had limited maneuverability close to shore and always ran the risk of running on uncharted rocks and shoals. Ironically, these were the very features Des Barres was supposed to investigate. Des Barres soon discovered his smaller boats easily swamped in the unpredictable conditions of the North Atlantic. Once, he barely escaped drowning when landing on the treacherous shores of Sable Island in 1767.

The *Atlantic Neptune*

Halfway through *Canceaux*'s survey, an important meeting occurred in the village of Liverpool, Nova Scotia, on August 10, 1770. Samuel Holland and Joseph Des Barres had corresponded over the years, but this was the first time they had seen each other since the survey project began in 1764. Mowat noted the event in the ship's log.

Canceaux was the first to arrive at Liverpool:

> *Saw entrance of Liverpool Harbor at 4:00 PM and fired six guns as a signal for Mr. Des Barres surveying schooner to come into Liverpool Harbor at 8:00 PM. Anchored at 11:00 PM on the eastern shore. Two survey schooners and one large cutter was with his party.*

The meeting lasted for three days and took place at the home of Simeon Perkins, a local merchant. At the Liverpool meeting, Samuel Holland made a dramatic proposal to Joseph Des Barres. His idea was the two men combine forces and publish their surveys as a unified work. The result would be several volumes of charts of North America.

Stephen Hornsby wrote, "In essence the two surveyors laid the foundations for *The Atlantic Neptune*." Des Barres was initially reluctant "to join the work of others to mine," but he soon realized how Holland's proposal would further his career. Although Henry Mowat was present at the meeting, we do not know the extent to which he was involved in the conversations that ensued.

Holland's plan was that he would provide the land surveys and that Des Barres would provide the sea charts. However, there was still much work to be done. For example, more soundings and surveys were needed, especially in the Gulf of St. Lawrence. The agreement, however, was that Des Barres would publish a nautical atlas fully acknowledging Holland's role.

After securing the approval of the admiralty for the scheme, Des Barres returned to England in 1774 and toiled for ten years to organize and

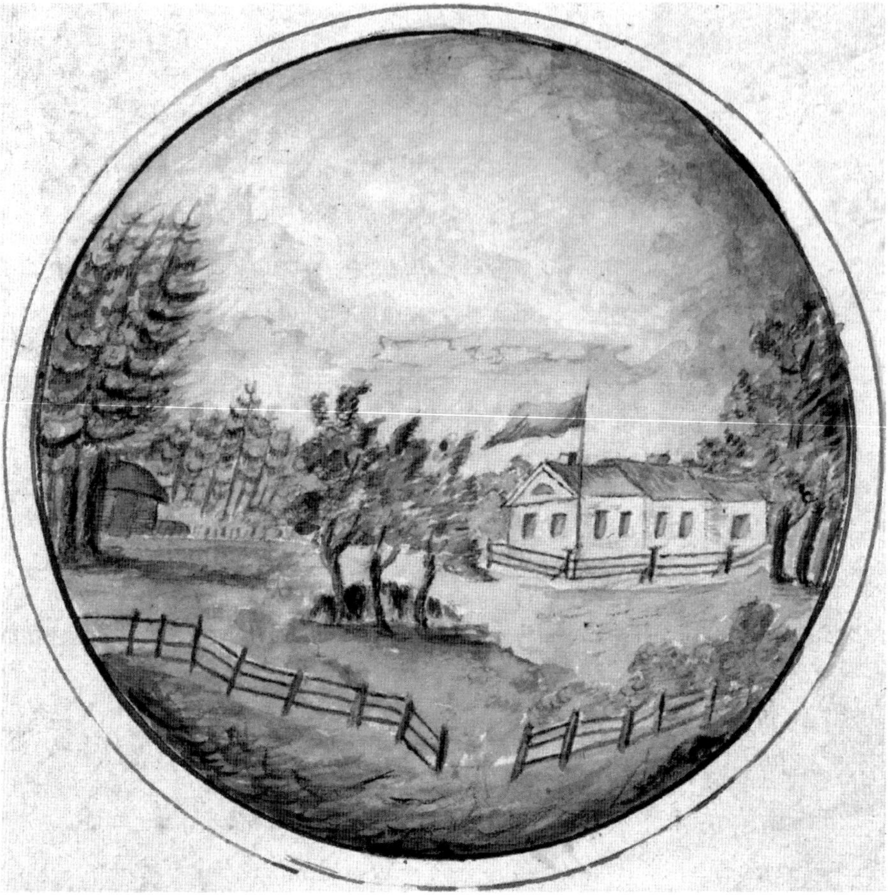

Joseph Des Barres frequently worked on his charts and drawings for the *Atlantic Neptune* project at his estate, Castle Frederick, near Falmouth, Nova Scotia. *Courtesy of the Library and Archives of Canada.*

update his "charts and views" [illustrations] into publishable form. Des Barres and the admiralty published the opus jointly between 1774 and 1784. Although the title page of *Atlantic Neptune* states that Des Barres was the publisher, Holland's contributions were acknowledged on the cover of the volume *Charts of the Coast and Harbors in the Gulph and River of St. Lawrence*.

Meanwhile, Samuel Holland continued his survey of the New England coast. He was finally ordered back to England in 1775 due to worsening relations with the American colonies.

The *Atlantic Neptune* was the first marine atlas to contain comprehensive charts and views of the North American coast as well as hydrographical and topographical details. Stephen Hornsby wrote in *Surveyors of Empire*, "Judged by modern standards, many of the charts in the *Atlantic Neptune* were remarkably accurate."

Samuel Holland returned to North America in the middle of the American Revolution and spent the rest of his life in Quebec. He was the first lieutenant governor of Upper Canada and continued to survey and lay out townships until his death in 1801 at the age of seventy-three. Stephen Hornsby provides an appropriate epitaph: "He died knowing that he had surveyed and mapped more of North America than anyone else."

After the Revolution, Joseph Des Barres was appointed lieutenant governor of Cape Breton Island and subsequently lieutenant governor of Prince Edward Island. Des Barres's long life came to an end in 1824 when he died in Halifax, Nova Scotia, at the age of 102.

Chapter 3

The Revolution Begins in Maine

You may perceive that the Rebels of the Continent are indefatigable in spreading their poison.
—British Admiral Samuel Graves

Henry Mowat's reputation among Mainers took a turn for the worse in 1775. Prior to this, he was known as a knowledgeable sailor and surveyor, if an overly aggressive pursuer of smugglers. By the end of the year, the name Mowat had been connected to two significant altercations with Mainers. The first, although a case of mistaken identity, would darken his name; the second, the burning of Falmouth, would condemn him to two centuries of vilification.

Beginning with the Intolerable Acts, also known as the Coercive Acts, issued in 1774, relations between the Crown and Massachusetts colonists steadily grew worse. The severe measures were issued by Parliament in response to the Boston Tea Party, which had occurred in December 1773. By making an example of Massachusetts (which included the Province of Maine), the British Parliament hoped these punitive measures would reverse the trend of colonial resistance to parliamentary authority that had begun with the Stamp Act in 1765.

Interestingly, the various Intolerable Acts hurt Mainers more than the people of Massachusetts. The Boston Port Act closed the port to colonial vessels carrying "any merchandise whatsoever" except those carrying food or firewood to Boston. Colin Woodard wrote in *The Lobster Coast*, "The

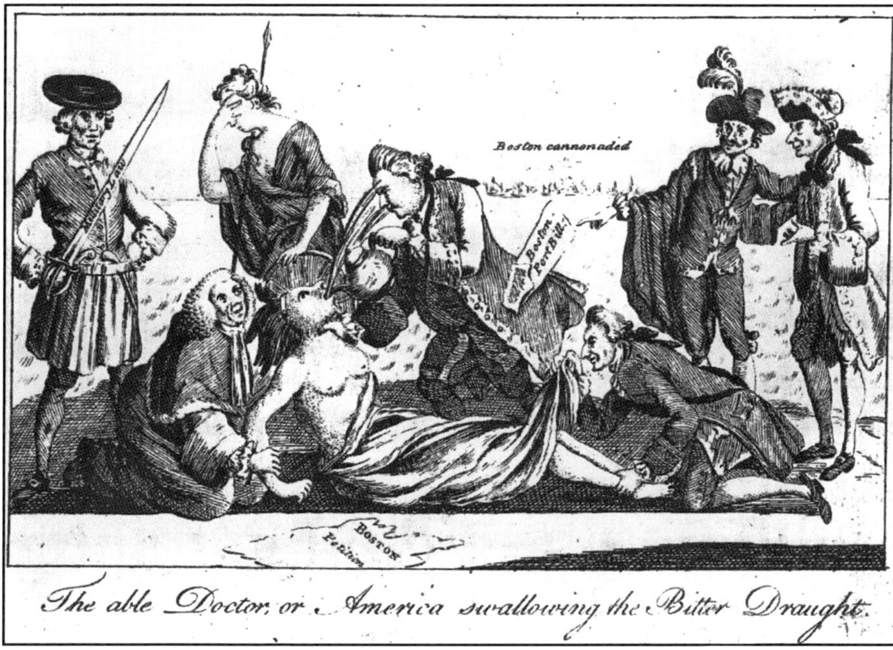

This cartoon depicting the Intolerable Acts was copied and distributed throughout the thirteen colonies shortly before the Revolution. *Courtesy of Wikipedia.*

measure was harmful to Boston, but disastrous for Maine towns, where the economy was almost completely dependent on trade with the colonial capital." Many colonists saw the Intolerable/Coercive Acts as a violation of their constitutional rights as granted by their colonial charters.

Woodard adds:

> *Downeast Mainers faced malnutrition as they imported much of their food and supplies form Boston and could not raise their own on the rocky soil. The fact that certain loyalist merchant princes could continue shipping food, firewood and other military supplies to the city from other ports earned them the lasting wrath of their poorer, suffering neighbors. The situation proved explosive.*

The Massachusetts Government Act provoked even more outrage than the Port Act because it altered the government of Massachusetts and brought it directly under control of the military governor of Boston, General Gage. Under the terms of the Government Act, the king or Massachusetts governor General Gage would appoint all positions in the colonial government.

For several years, Henry Mowat in *Canceaux* had voyaged along the New England coast in this deteriorating atmosphere. Clearly Mowat was aware of growing hostile feelings, and *Canceaux*'s log refers to "exercising the marines on shore" as early as September 27, 1771. Marines had been on board *Canceaux* for a number of years, although this was the first mention of their becoming an active presence.

By now, marines were a part of every ship's company, usually in the ratio of about one to every four sailors. With the onboard discipline problems described in the logs by Mowat, marines originally acted as guards to the officers and enforcers of their authority. As relations between the British and the American colonists worsened, marines acted as a police force both aboard ship and ashore.

In *Canceaux*'s emerging role as a guardian of British interests, it is clear that as the ship's captain, Mowat realized the importance of keeping his ship in a state of readiness for combat. By the fall of 1773, there are almost daily references in the log to "exercising the people at the Great Guns and Small arms."

As the situation grew increasingly tense around Boston, *Canceaux* spent much of the summer and fall of 1774 in the harbor "showing the flag." This included guarding British merchant ships, transporting British troops around the harbor and generally making the population of Boston aware of a military presence. The ship's log continued to make frequent references to "exercising the people at great guns and small arms."

By the time the Battles of Lexington and Concord occurred in April 1775, *Canceaux* had moved to Falmouth (Portland), also known as Falmouth Neck. Interestingly, there was no reaction to these conflicts in the ship's log by Captain Mowat. Meanwhile, the situation continued to unravel in Boston and elsewhere throughout the spring and summer of 1775.

A Case of Tonypandy: Henry Mowat and the Dismantling of Fort Pownall

Before proceeding, it is appropriate to examine a curious situation that did not directly involve Henry Mowat but one that has created a certain amount of historical confusion regarding his reputation for the past two hundred years.

Tonypandy is a village in Wales. In the early twentieth century there was a nasty clash between striking coal miners and the police. Shots were allegedly

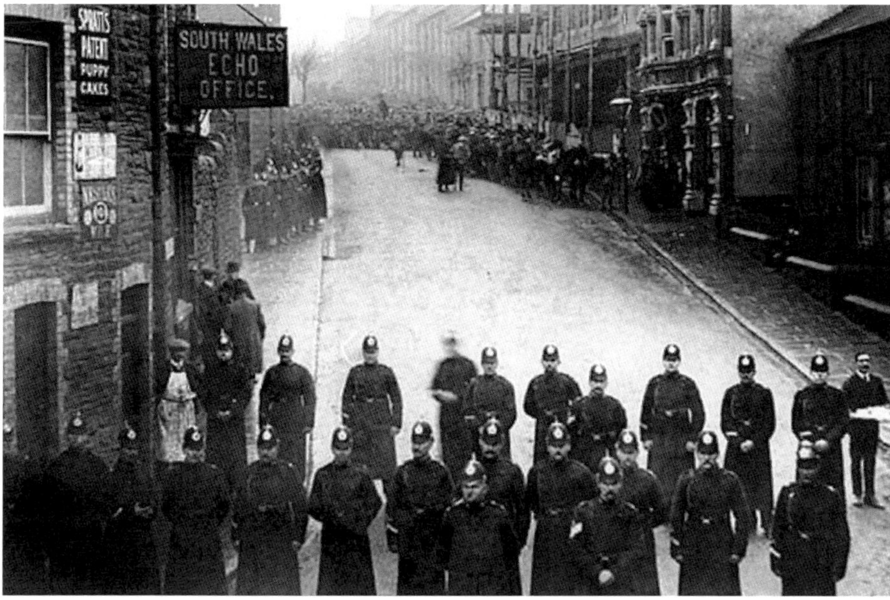

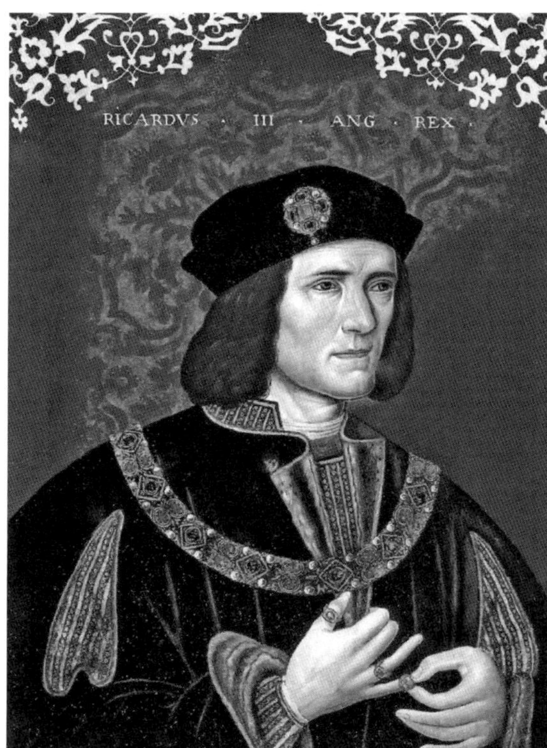

Above: Striking Welsh miners met the police in the town square of Tonypandy, Wales, in 1910. *Courtesy of Wikipedia.*

Right: Josephine Tey used Richard III's alleged murder of his nephews as an example of Tonypandy in her book *The Daughter of Time*. *Courtesy of Wikipedia.*

fired, and a number of miners were reportedly killed. The facts of the story, however, were quite different. A subsequent investigation revealed that very few miners or soldiers were injured and that none were killed. Nevertheless, for the past hundred years, Tonypandy has become shorthand for a widely accepted historical myth.

Josephine Tey used the episode as the basis for her mystery classic *The Daughter of Time*, which she wrote in 1951. The title comes from a quote by Francis Bacon, "Truth is the daughter of time, not of authority." In her book, Tey was exploring how history is constructed and how certain versions of events come to be widely accepted as the truth, despite a lack of evidence. In this case, she was using the example of how Richard III was accused of murdering his two nephews.

Like Richard III, who Tey absolves of the murders in her novel, Henry Mowat was erroneously blamed for a "wicked" action by Mainers that occurred at the beginning of the Revolutionary War. In Mowat's case, he was thought to be responsible for dismantling Fort Pownall at the mouth of the Penobscot River. Mowat and his ship *Canceaux* had been a familiar British presence in Maine waters since 1764, so his was an example of guilt by association. But was he guilty?

Mowat deserved notoriety for his burning of Falmouth in October 1775. And his involvement in the destruction the American fleet at Penobscot Bay in 1779 added to his reputation as the "Scourge of Maine" during the Revolution. An examination of the facts surrounding the dismantling of Fort Pownall, however, reveals a different tale.

William D. Williamson was the second governor of Maine, a United States congressman and a prominent nineteenth-century Maine historian. Williamson published the two-volume *History of the State of Maine* in the late 1830s, which stood as the standard reference on early Maine history for the rest of the nineteenth century. In his second volume, Williamson erroneously credited the "pacification" of the fort to Henry Mowat. "Mowat proceeding next to Penobscot, dismantled Fort Pownall, carried away the guns and ammunition, and nearly destroyed the rich trade with the natives. He then returned to Falmouth Harbor." Because Williamson jumped to the conclusion that Mowat was the responsible party, subsequent historians followed his lead.

Nineteenth-century Maine historians, and at least one writer in the twenty-first century, have continued to assume that Captain Mowat was responsible for most of the hostile actions taken by the British navy that occurred in Maine during the Revolution. In the case of the destruction of

Fort Pownall, it will be shown that Mowat was blameless. Before explaining his role, however, it is important to examine the circumstances surrounding the building of Fort Pownall.

Governor Thomas Pownall wrote a letter to British prime minister William Pitt in 1758 in which he citied the advantages of building a fort on Wasaumkeag Point, now known as Fort Point:

> *A Fort at Penobscot River would be of utmost importance. It would take possession of the very fine Country. It would effectively drive off the remains of the Noridgwoak and Penobscot Indians, as it would break up their hunting and fishing. It would take possession of the finest bay in North America for large shipping just at the south of the Bay of Fundy and would be advancing the frontiers of his Majesty's Dominions.*

Governor Pownall hoped to encourage English settlers to move into the region, as fears of a French and Indian attack were diminishing in the area. Indeed they were. The next year, many of the men who had helped build the fort returned to Massachusetts and gave glowing reports of the benefits of settling in the area.

The fort's strategic location soon began to attract immigrants to this new frontier. Between 1760 and 1772, a tide of settlers flowed into the lands between Camden and Bangor on the western side of the Penobscot River and between Castine and Brewer on its eastern shores. By the early 1770s, the population around Fort Pownall had grown substantially and six townships had been established along the river. At the same time, the newly arrived settlers continued to depend heavily on the security and economic support provided by the fort.

Rufus Buck writes in *A History of the Town of Bucksport*, "The Indians signified their intention to enjoy the friendship and receive the protection of our forces." Buck adds, "A large traffic was carried on for several years subsequent to the war, the natives receiving all the supplies needed by them in exchange for the furs and articles of their own production."

Revolutionary War veteran Joseph Martin gives a description of the fort:

> *It was a regular fortification with a blockhouse in the center, surrounded by a ditch, fifteen feet wide at the top. The bloc* [sic] *house was of square timber two stories high. In the upper room were ten or twelve cannon. The houses of the officers were situated between the fort and the bank of the river.*

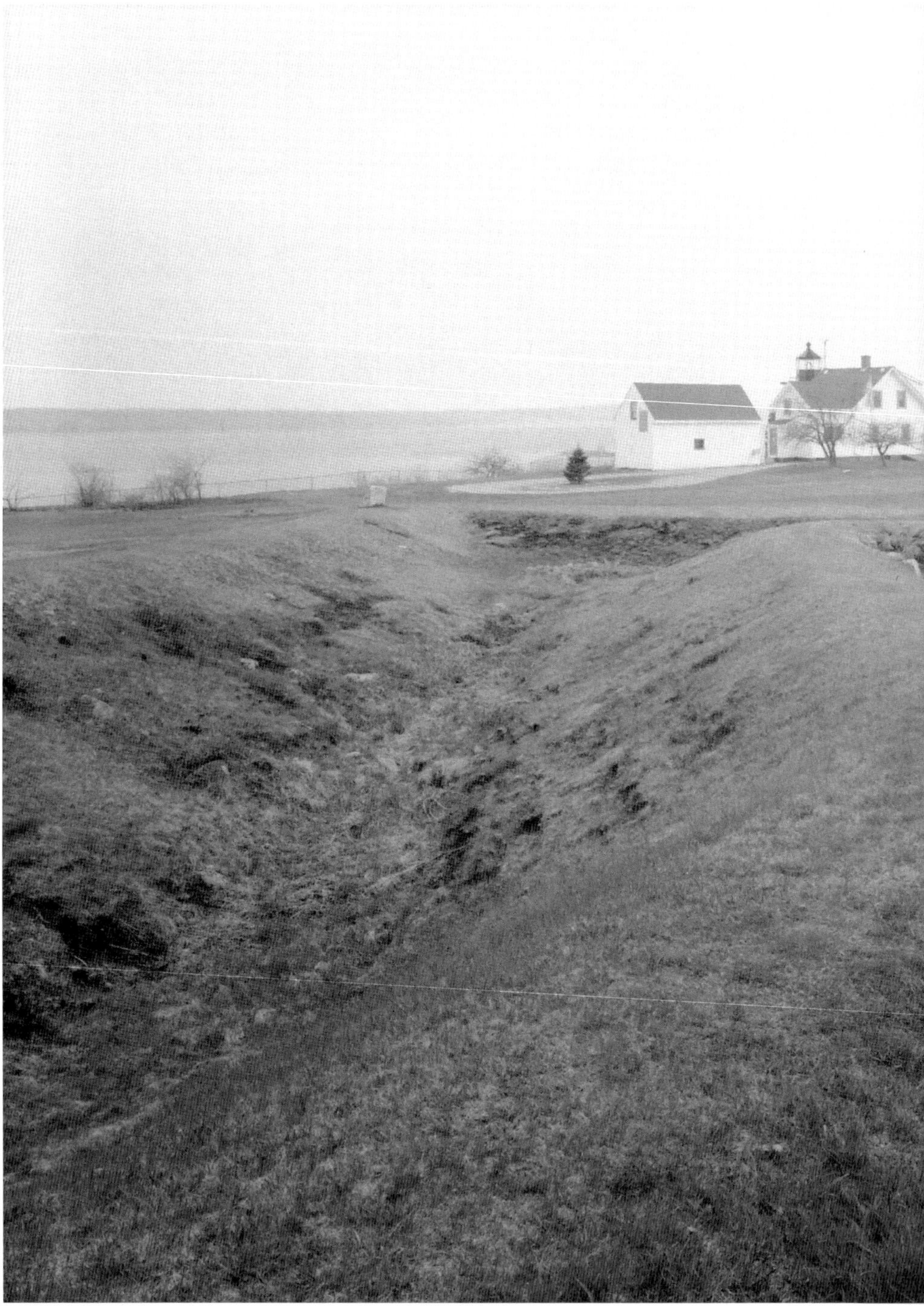

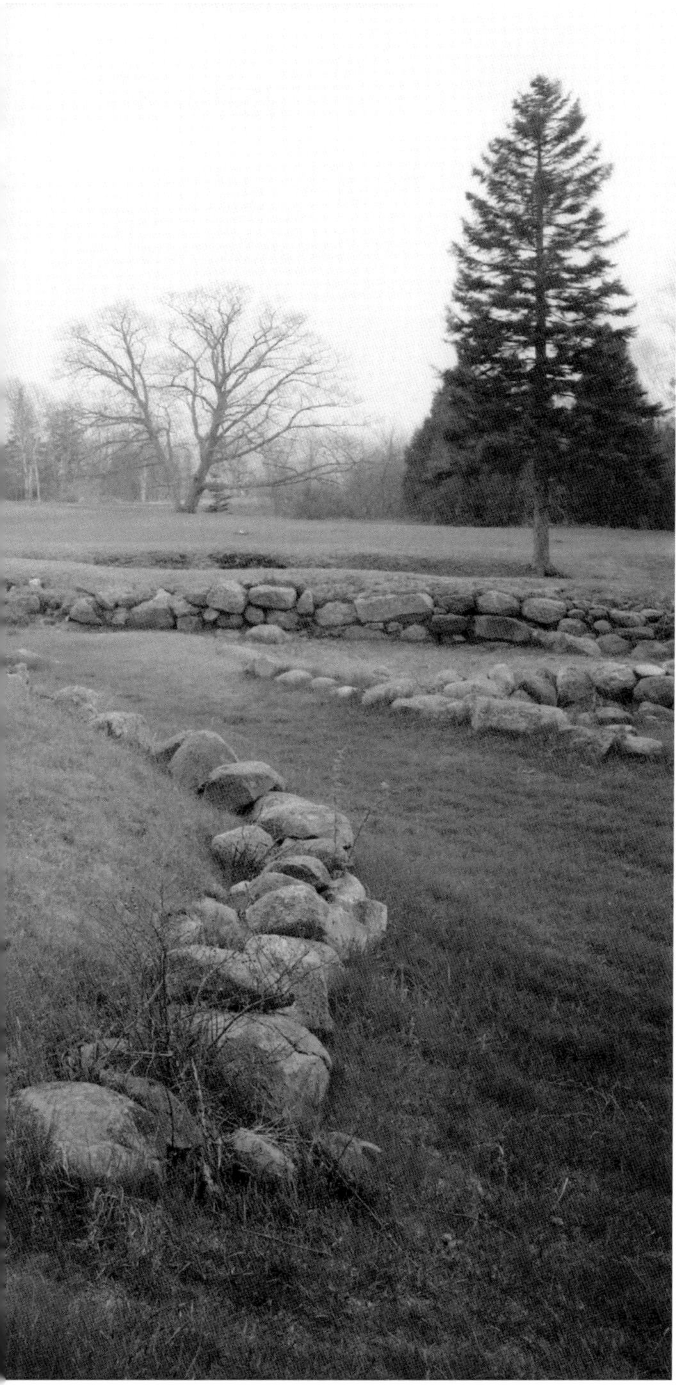

The walls of Fort Pownall in the foreground. The ranger station and Penobscot River are in the background. *Courtesy of the Library of Congress.*

As trade with Indians began to flourish, another large building was erected near the fort, "to accommodate public worship, and to shelter the natives in stormy weather," Buck tells us. It was estimated that over seven hundred Indians came to Fort Pownall "for the purpose of trade," and that the storerooms were filled with "the best quality of furs, beaver, otter and sable."

Until the Revolutionary War broke out, the fort's garrison consisted of a commander, a lieutenant, a gunner, an armorer, an interpreter and a detachment of privates. General Jedediah Preble from Falmouth was the fort's first commander. It is interesting that one of his sons was Commodore Edward Preble, who would go on to have a distinguished career as a United States naval officer.

Meanwhile in Massachusetts, tensions were continuing to escalate between the British authorities and the rebellious citizens of Boston. In Maine, one effect of this was that Massachusetts Governor Hutchinson, a zealous supporter of the King, appointed a Tory sympathizer, Thomas Goldthwait, to replace John Preble as commander of the fort. (Preble was another of Jedediah's sons.)

Fort Pownall's crisis was now at hand. During this period, according to Rufus Buck, "The inhabitants [of the area] suffered extremely for want of provisions, the spring [of 1775] was unusually dry and the whole summer so cold that no corn and but little grain of any kind was raised in the region of the Penobscot River." Buck adds, "Had it not been for the public store house of provisions the people would have perished from hunger."

We have evidence from *Canceaux*'s log that Henry Mowat was in Falmouth Harbor from April 8 until the end of the month. We also know from accounts by soldiers at Fort Pownall that a British force sacked the fort on April 14, 1775. It is hard to be in two places at the same time, and in this case, the log makes it clear that on April 14, the day of the dismantling, Mowat was on his ship in Falmouth. In fact, he recorded "strong gales and squally with snow, 8 AM, loosed sails to dry."

If Henry Mowat didn't do the deed, then who dismantled Fort Pownall? Maine historian Robert Brook wrote "The Pacification of Fort Pownall" in 1975 to commemorate the 200th anniversary of the event. In the article, he establishes that the commander of the Fort Pownall expedition was Lieutenant Thomas Graves, who later distinguished himself as an admiral at the battle of Copenhagen in 1800. Lieutenant Graves was the nephew of Vice Admiral Samuel Graves, commander of the British North American squadron.

Robert Brook cites a letter written by Massachusetts governor General Thomas Gage to Admiral Graves, which states, "I take the liberty to inquire of you whether you have a ship or armed vessel at or near the Penobscot River that could be sent there [to Fort Pownall] on temporary service?" As a result of the rapid escalation of the conflict around Boston, both sides were desperately seeking to gain control of all available arms and ammunition. One result of this had serious consequences for Fort Pownall.

Following a meeting between the two commanders, the decision was made to "pacify" the fort. General Gage sent a letter with Lieutenant Graves to give to the fort's commander, Thomas Goldthwait. "Take on board all the artillery and spare arms belonging to and in store at said fort. This is to require you to deliver said artillery and spare arms into the charge of Lieutenant Graves."

Lieutenant Graves sailed the armed schooner *Diana*, in the company of the schooner *Neptune*—which carried a detachment of soldiers from the Sixty-Fourth regiment—heading for the Penobscot River on April 9, 1775. Their orders were to "dismantle the fort and seize the cannon ammunition and stores and proceed to Falmouth." *Diana*'s log was lost when the Americans burned the ship during a battle outside Boston Harbor in May 1775, but we have an account by William Molineux, a soldier at Fort Pownall, describing what happened.

> *On Friday evening April 13th came to the Penobscot River a top-sail schooner which anchored near Fort Pownall which myself and others took to be a merchantman going up the river to purchase lumber and early the next morning we saw another schooner which came too and anchored near the other. Soon after came ashore some sailors to beg some milk for their breakfast. Presently after came on shore an officer who enquired for the commander of the fort and on seeing him presented an order from General Gage for the cannon and spare arms. He then returned on board and immediately appeared a large number of soldiers on the deck (which had not before been seen) who directly got into boats and came ashore, marched into the fort and went to work getting out the cannon which was carried on board.*

Molineux added that he did not think the fort's commander, Thomas Goldthwait, could have resisted the order. "I would further add that the officer which commanded the party said that had Colonel Goldthwait refurst, it was his orders to destroy the fort immediately."

The list of what was taken included eight cannon; two mortars, with shot and canisters; and forty-five small arms with ammunition. Thus Fort Pownall ceased to function as an armed garrison on April 15, 1775. Goldthwait was criticized for surrendering so easily, and he later protested the action by writing to General Gage. It was clear, however, that his small force of six or seven men would have been easily overwhelmed and the fort destroyed.

In an interesting postscript to the event, there is an entry in *Canceaux*'s log written by Mowat on April 25. "PM came in here [Falmouth] his Majesties schooner *Diana* and the *Neptune* schooner belonging to General Gage with an officer and party on board belonging to the 46th regiment." The next day the log reported, "PM sailed hence the two schooners for Boston." It is reasonable to assume that the two ships were returning to Boston with arms and artillery they had taken from Fort Pownall on April 15.

Reputations, however, die hard. Seventy-seven years later, Rufus Buck, having read Williamson's account of the disarmament of Fort Pownall, picked up the Tonypandy theme. Buck refers to Mowat in his *History of the Town of Bucksport* in 1857 when writing about the events in April 1775:

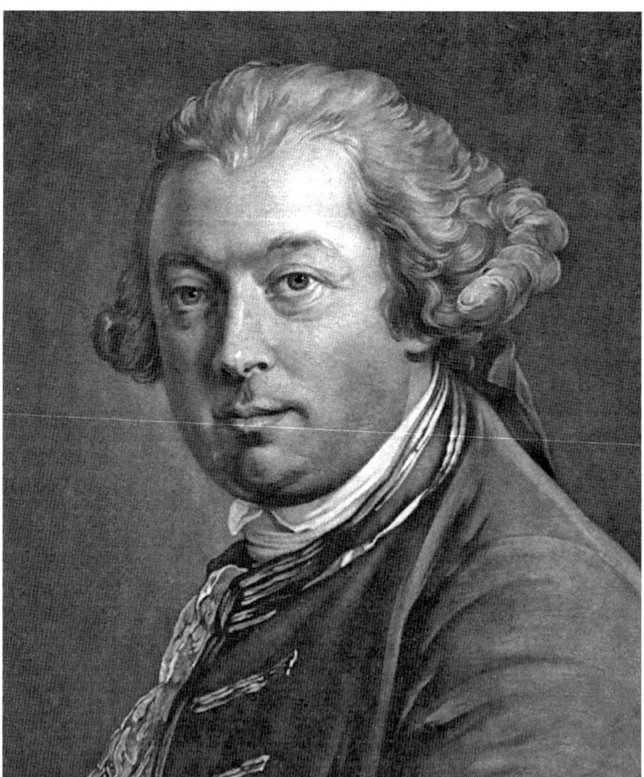

The fort was named after Thomas Pownall, a British politician and colonial official who was governor of the Province of Massachusetts Bay from 1757 to 1760. When he returned to England, Pownall was a member of Parliament. *Courtesy of Wikipedia.*

> *Colonal Mowatt with a British ship of war touched at Fort Pownall and completely dismantled it, carrying away all the arms and moveables. From this time the trade was broken up which had been profitably improved for over 20 years.*

George Varney continues the refrain in his *History of Waldo County* in 1886. "Neither of these actions [Lexington and Concord and Bunker Hill] was the occasion of so much anxiety as the dismantling of Fort Pownall by Mowatt in April of the same year…His actions brought down upon him the wrath of the settlers."

Most recently, maritime historian Louis Arthur Norton wrote an article in 2007, "Henry Mowat: Miscreant of the Maine Coast," in which he also blamed Mowat for demolishing of Fort Pownall:

> *On the eve of the American Revolution loyalist Colonel Thomas Goldthwait, then in command of Fort Pownall, allowed Mowat and his men on the* Canceaux *to remove the fort's cannons and powder to keep them out of insurgent's hands. In retaliation, a regiment of American rebels burned down the blockhouse and filled in the fort's ditch like moat to prevent the British reoccupation of the fort. The dismantling of Fort Pownall was the first of three vents that contributed to Mainers' frustrations with Henry Mowat and his role in the Revolution.*

The dismantling of the fort and surrounding buildings left the people in the area destitute and anxious. The result was a significant worsening in the relationship between the Crown and coastal Mainers. What had become a thriving settlement was reduced to a starving community fearful of the return of hostile Indians.

During the remainder of 1775, Henry Mowat's reputation would change from that of somewhat controversial Scottish sea captain to a more menacing presence for which he would be known during and after the Revolution.

Samuel Thompson's War

Shortly after Fort Pownall was dismantled, Captain Mowat was involved in a little scrap known as Thompson's War. *Canceaux*'s log makes a number of references to the subject.

The cause of Thompson's War goes back to the imposition of the Intolerable Acts issued in 1774, which prohibited colonists from selling their goods to Boston. The provincial congress in Massachusetts responded by declaring an embargo on trade with the British, which would deprive their navy of food and naval stores. The question of enforcement for both sides was where problems arose.

Samuel Thompson was a volatile innkeeper from Brunswick, in the Province of Maine, appointed to administer the embargo in his district by the provincial congress. In retrospect, Thompson's approach to enforcing the embargo undoubtedly escalated the situation. In a lecture he gave at the Maine Historical Society in 1903, Nathan Goold stated, "It was such as he who made the beginning and the end of the Revolution possible."

The vehement and revolutionary Thompson was an ardent member of the Sons of Liberty and a man of considerable wealth for his time. Regarding his private life, it is known only that his wife was mentally unstable and that she killed their five-year-old adopted son. Apparently another of their children was severely retarded. Under the circumstances, it seems likely that Thompson's home life was not a happy or stable environment.

After the Boston Tea Party, Thompson had led an expedition of armed supporters, in December 1773, on a foray up the Kennebec River in 1774. Their purpose was to enforce the colonial embargo against suspected Tories, but things quickly got out of hand. The houses of merchants were searched, and any tea discovered was thrown in the river. A Mr. Gardiner describes a mob of men "raging up the river by force of arms, destroying one hundred and fifty pounds of tea and his life being threatened with the utmost vengeance." Several gallons of rum were stolen and consumed, and a Mr. Hazard was thrown in the river after being robbed.

The colorful Thompson was a man whose personality dominated a room the minute he entered. Nathan Goold gives us a description of this prominent and ardent patriot:

> *A portly man, not tall, somewhat corpulent, and with a robust constitution. He was rather fierce in appearance, had strong mental powers, was witty in conversation and was a man of capacity. He was a substantial citizen, but he made many enemies as such men do, who have positive convictions and do not hesitate to declare them at the time of exciting events.*

Goold relates that Thomson once heard a person say what a pity it was he had no better education. Turning, Thompson replied, "If I have no education perhaps I can furnish some ideas to those who have." A member of the general court once told him that if he had an education he would have been a great man to which Thompson responded, "If I had your education I would have put you in my pocket."

George and Henry Wheeler wrote in *The History of Brunswick*:

> *He* [Thompson] *possessed no mean power of debate and could express himself tersely and vigorously. He was impetuous, noisy and sometimes even furious…Notwithstanding the anecdotes tending to throw ridicule upon him, it is evident that General Thompson must have been in some respects a remarkable man or he could not for so long a period have possessed the confidence of a majority of his fellow citizens and filled the responsible stations which he did. At all events, the strength of his patriotism ought to overshadow many minor defects of character.*

This was the man who was the leader of the committee of safety for his district and would escalate the situation by kidnapping Henry Mowat when he was in Falmouth. Prior to his confrontation with Mowat, Thompson had attended three sessions of the Massachusetts Provincial Congress in 1774 and 1775. Each time, he would return to Brunswick filled with zeal to vigorously carry out their directives. This included making his constituency aware of the actions of the congress, organizing the local militia and investigating those suspected of violating the embargo. High on Thompson's list of suspects was Edward Parry, a shipping agent for the king who lived in Bath.

Following the third provincial congress, Thompson was ordered "to repair immediately to the Casco Bay area and take the most effectual measures to acquaint the people that one Mr. Parry is in the eastern part of the country endeavoring to supply our enemies with masts, spars and timber." Thompson was directed to prevent people from aiding Parry in "procuring such articles."

Canceaux's log picks up the sequence of events at this point. Parry was appropriately fearful of what Thompson might do and wrote to Mowat asking for protection. Mowat's reply was that he would respond aggressively "to those detaining or interfering with you," and he told Parry to give him their names. "You may depend on me," he assured Parry.

The next correspondence recorded in *Canceaux*'s log is a letter to Mowat on May 2 signed by eighteen of the leading citizens of Falmouth,

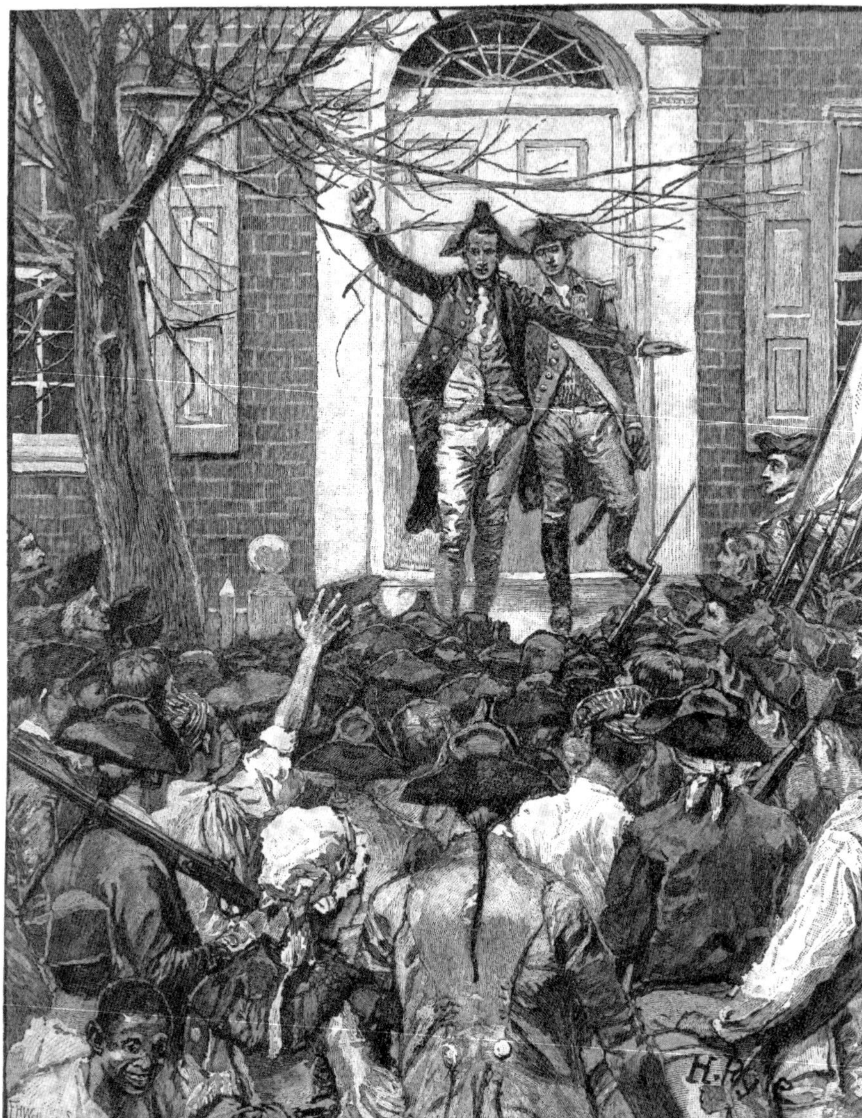

Samuel Thompson is shown speaking vehemently to the citizens of Falmouth, urging them to oppose the actions of the British government. *Courtesy of the Maine Historical Society.*

reassuring him of their loyalty to the Crown: "We have been relieved by your spirited conduct to persons who are obnoxious to the enemies of our happy Constitution and by your kind and courteous behavior to all friends of Government."

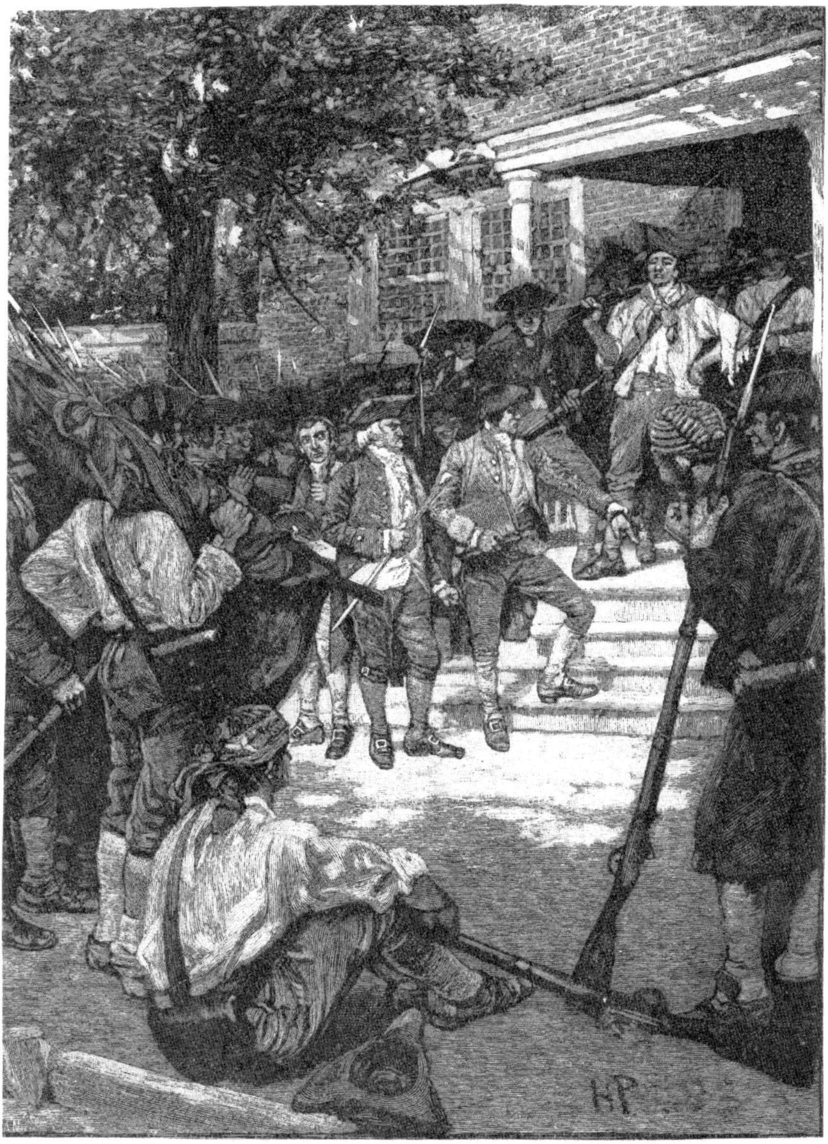

Samuel Thompson was a captivating speaker. Here he is seen addressing an attentive crowd. *Courtesy of the Maine Historical Society.*

At this point, another name enters the lists. Samuel Coulson was a Tory sea captain from Falmouth who was rigging his ship in preparation for sailing it to England with a load of masts, spars and timber. (Whether the cargo was Parry's is not clear.) In any case, the May 2 letter from the leading citizens to Mowat also begs that he not leave Falmouth, "when Captain Coulson's ship is ready for sea." The letter continued, "For this would leave us a prey to the sons of rapine and lawless violence. We further entreat you to represent our dangerous situation to General Gage and Admiral Graves."

Meanwhile, Thompson went to Bath "with twenty resolute men" and arrested Parry for violating the provincial congress embargo. Parry was forced to pay a fine of £2,000 while the congress deliberated on his fate. He was eventually tried and spent a year in jail before he was exchanged and sent to England.

Parry's and Coulson's were just two of a number of cases in which Thompson dealt ruthlessly with Loyalist sympathizers living in the Falmouth-Brunswick area. Another was John Bernard, a merchant and an associate of Parry's, who was also suspected of being a Tory. It is interesting that Bernard was the son of Francis Bernard, who had been governor of Massachusetts from 1760 to 1771. To complete the circle, the senior Bernard had preceded Thomas Pownall, the builder of Fort Pownall, as governor of Massachusetts. Bernard was later able to satisfy the general court of his loyalty to the colonial cause.

What happened next is not entirely clear 240 years later. One view was that Parry planned to load his cargo of naval stores on Coulson's ship at the Falmouth docks. Another was that Coulson already had a shipload of naval stores on board and he wanted to unload them in Falmouth. Against this background of the violation of the Non-Importation Act, the leading citizens of Falmouth met to consider what to do about Coulson. After a discussion, the committee voted not to allow him to unload the naval stores or, conversely, to load Parry's shipment. It was hoped this would appease the radical contingent led by Thompson.

Coulson then sailed to Boston, where he met with Admiral Graves and requested the continued assistance of Henry Mowat and *Canceaux* to protect his vessel in Falmouth. Coulson returned on May 9, which set the stage for Thompson's confrontation with Mowat.

Meanwhile, news of Lexington and Concord had reached Falmouth. Samuel Thompson wrote a letter to the Massachusetts General Court, portions of which follow.

> *We are all staunch for Country, except for three men, one of them deserted, the other two are in irons. As for the vessels which attempted to convey stuff to our enemies, they have been stopped, and I am about*

> *to move about two hundred white pine masts and other stuff gotten for our enemies use. Having heard of the cruel murders* [Lexington and Concord] *they have done in our province, makes us more resolute than ever finding that the sword is drawn first on their side...Sir, as powder and guns is much wanted in these parts also provision, have your thoughts something in this matter.*

The Massachusetts Council immediately directed that a barrel of gunpowder be delivered to Thompson, and he had it distributed to local patriot captains as a defense against the patrolling British ships. Apparently *Canceaux* was particularly resented. As Goold described the situation, "The British vessels then cruising along our coast were a constant menace. They impressed [seized] fishermen and appropriated their stores. The insolence of the British officers was almost unbearable and none was more sincerely hated than Henry Mowat."

It has been previously noted that for much of April, Mowat was at Falmouth Harbor where one of his responsibilities was to protect Thomas Coulson as he rigged his ship. During this time, the scheming Thompson concocted a plan to capture *Canceaux*. His idea was to obtain a ship that was large enough to carry sixty or seventy men and disguise it as a wooden coaster (a merchant vessel carrying wood). With his men hiding in the hold, Thompson planned to go alongside *Canceaux* at night, surprise the crew and seize the British ship.

Henry Mowat includes a letter in *Canceaux*'s log that he wrote to Admiral Graves on May 4, which includes his description of the worsening situation:

> *The greater part of the people in this part of the country have been under arms constantly threatening destruction to the persons and properties of those who refuse to join them. In Brunswick they laid hold of five of the Friends of Government* [Loyalists] *one of which they buried alive and put the rest in jail.* [In Falmouth] *they resolved to embark two sloops in order to burn* Canceaux [but] *the town disapproved of the plan and refused assistance.*

Both accounts agree that when word of Thompson's audacious plan leaked out, a majority of the citizens of Falmouth were horrified, fearing retaliation by the British. Enoch Freeman, one of the town fathers, wrote Thompson asking him to abandon the scheme, which, for the moment, he did.

Samuel Thompson was still determined to take some kind of action, and he waited impatiently for the right opportunity. He and fifty men hid in the woods on Munjoy Hill, overlooking Falmouth Harbor, on May 8 to await developments.

Thinking that the situation had calmed down, Henry Mowat had gone ashore to arrange church services for his crew the next day, which was a Sunday. He was walking on Munjoy Hill with the Tory Anglican minister John Wiswall and *Canceaux*'s surgeon, Dr. Baillie, when they were spotted and captured by three of Thompson's men. The "interception," as *Canceaux*'s log describes the event, took place on the afternoon of May 9.

The prisoners were brought to Thompson, at which point Mowat handed over his sword. It was returned, but Thompson's War was underway. When word of Thompson's reckless action reached Falmouth, fear spread among the citizens, who feared retaliation by *Canceaux*, which was moored in the harbor. The rebel camp was quickly visited by a number of prominent citizens who strongly urged that Mowat be released.

It should be emphasized that at this point most of the citizens of Falmouth, if not outright Loyalists, were more moderate patriots compared to the radical Thompson and his men. As the news spread, hundreds of militiamen poured into Falmouth from nearby Gorham, Cape Elizabeth, Scarborough and Windham, ready to prevent Mowat's rescue by sympathetic townspeople who were fearful of British retaliation. Clearly there was a considerable gap between the rich and relatively well-to-do citizens of Falmouth, who favored releasing Mowat, and those who were less well off, from the villages and farms in the surrounding area.

Thompson initially refused to release Mowat, and he was taken to Marston's Tavern, which stood in what is now Monument Square in Portland. In the harbor on *Canceaux*, Mowat's sailing master, Lieutenant Hogg, threatened to burn the town if Mowat was not released within two hours. Two companies of volunteers were drawn up in front of the tavern defying Hogg as Thompson's War intensified.

Thompson's response to Hogg was, "Fire away! Fire away, every gun you fire I will cut off a joint." Two salutes (gunpowder charges without shot) were fired from *Canceaux*, although Mowat's fingers remained intact. (There is a possibility that they were live rounds.) Real or not, the effects of the gunfire, however, frightened many of the women and children in the town to such a degree that some crawled under the wharves, ran into cellars or out of town. "Such a shrieking scene was never before presented to view here," Nathan Goold related.

Prominent citizens, led by General Jedediah Preble and Enoch Freeman, renewed their efforts to release Mowat. Thompson finally agreed—perhaps he wasn't sure what to do with his captive—and the prisoners were freed on parole at 9:00 p.m. As he departed, Mowat profusely thanked the "respectable inhabitants" for their help in saving his life, and he promised to return from *Canceaux* the following morning at 9:00 a.m.

It was no great surprise that the next morning Henry Mowat decided not to honor the agreement. (Apparently some of his sailors who were ashore had overheard talk of a plot to kill their captain.) Mowat's prudent decision, however, caused a tumultuous scene in Falmouth that was primarily directed against Preble and Freeman, the two men who had vouched for Mowat's parole.

Colonel Thompson demanded that Preble and Freeman provide "refreshment" for his troops to atone for Mowat's absence. When they paid what amounted to a ransom of £14, they were released. Thompson next insisted that the two pay for the time and expense of assembling the militia, which amounted to £160. This they refused to do. Enraged and frustrated, Thompson let his men run amuck in Falmouth for the next few days.

To give us some perspective on Thompson's actions, Enoch Freeman, chairman of the Committee of Safety of Falmouth, wrote his son Samuel, who was a member of the provincial congress, on May 10:

> *We are in confusion though Colonel Thompson wrote us he had laid aside the scheme to take the ship* Canceaux. *Yet he appeared yesterday on the back of Falmouth Neck. I cannot help thinking that this is a very imprudent action and fear it will bring on the destruction of the town.*
>
> *Pray let Congress be informed of this affair and let us know whether Thompson had such orders. And pray the Congress give us directions for we are in such confusion nobody seems to be rational.*

Class warfare had come to Falmouth, which in this case was called Thompson's War. The town was taken over by hundreds of drunken militiamen who exacted tribute from the upstanding, more conservative members of the community. They seized all the goods they could find belonging to Coulson, Preble and others who they considered Tory sympathizers. At the waterfront, shots were fired at *Canceaux*, and one of Coulson's boats was stolen.

The same day, May 10, the *Canceaux* log records a frantic letter Mowat received from Edward Parry, which described his treatment by Thompson and his "illiterates." It relates how his offices were sacked, how he was made a prisoner and forced to pay a bail bond of £2,000 and remove his masts, etc. "Nor should he write to any officer of the navy or army for protection."

The log continued:

> *May 11th: The town full of armed men threatening destruction to the ship and plundering the town. Several men* [Reverend John Wiswall and George Lyde, Collector of Customs] *came on board* Canceaux *for protection.*
> *May 12th: Watched the motion of the Rebels. Fired several shot at different craft to bring them to. Heard the Rebels had begun to disperse.*
> *May 13th: The rebels began to disperse—fired three shots at two sloops but they got off.*
> *May 14th: Employed watching the motions of the Rebels.*

As illustrated by the log, it took several days for the rioting to subside, but after four days, most of the soldiers turned looters had gone home. They departed, sneering at the "Falmouth gentry" and saying that "the town ought to be laid in ashes," according to Nathan Goold.

Following the departure of the militia, the next day, May 15, Mowat sailed to Portsmouth with his ship filled with Falmouth Tories, including Coulson and Wiswall. The Anglican minister of Falmouth, John Wiswall, was so badly shaken by his capture and mistreatment by Thompson's men that he had already sought refuge on *Canceaux* on Saturday, May 14. From the ship, he sent word to his congregants that any who wished to hear him preach on the Sabbath could come on board and hear him. None went. Wiswall would later resign his position as minister of the Falmouth Anglican church and send word to his family to join him in the safer confines of Boston.

Thus did Thompson's War come to an end, signaling, as it did, the beginning of a larger conflict. It was not, as we shall see, an event that Henry Mowat would soon forget.

Enoch Freeman did not forget the event either, and on May 15, he addressed a second letter to the provincial congress in Massachusetts:

> *The alarming attempt of Colonel Thompson to take the ship* Canceaux *and Captain Henry Mowat has occasioned very great uneasiness in this town as it has a tendency to bring on certain ruin. We think Colonel Thompson's attempt was rash and injurious, if not unjustifiable, as we cannot learn he had any authority from you or the Congress.*

Responding to the concerns expressed by Enoch Freeman and others, the provincial congress sent Samuel Thompson the following directive on May 18, 1775:

> *This Congress has received information that the Committee of Correspondence of Falmouth on hearing that you were about making an attack on* Canceaux, *a man of war lying in the harbor of that town, decreed you to forbear any proceedings of that kind which you promised to do, but that you afterwards took the Captain of the ship of war and detained the Honorable Jedediah Preble and Enoch Freeman as hostages and that you levied contributions of money and other things from the subjects there.*
>
> *Though the Congress approves of your general zeal for this Country, yet it appears that your conduct in taking the Captain of the ship against your promise, and your levying money, or other things of the people is by no means justifiable.*

Despite the reprimand, in August, Thompson, ever the ardent patriot, sent a letter to the provincial congress in Massachusetts proposing an invasion of Nova Scotia. He announced that the expedition would cost £5,000 and consist of one thousand men, four armed vessels and eight transports. The fleet would be made up at Machias and proceed to Halifax, "and capture all the Tories we can." It should be noted that George Washington disapproved of the scheme when he heard of it.

Samuel Thompson continued to represent his district as a member of the provincial congress for the remainder of 1775 and 1776. Although he failed to capture *Canceaux*, he appears to have suffered no loss of prestige. Thompson was commissioned a brigadier general in 1776, and in 1779, he raised troops for the ill-fated Penobscot expedition, where again he would encounter his nemesis Henry Mowat.

After the Revolution, Thompson moved to Topsham, Maine, in 1784 and was an immediate and vocal supporter of the province's attempt to separate from Massachusetts. He was a member of the Massachusetts Constitutional Convention in 1788 where he opposed ratification of the federal constitution because it lacked a bill of rights and supported slavery. Later in his life, Thompson donated part of his significant real estate holdings in Brunswick to Bowdoin College when the school was chartered in 1794.

At the end of his lecture on Samuel Thompson, Nathan Goold concluded by saying, "Had the effort for our independence been a failure

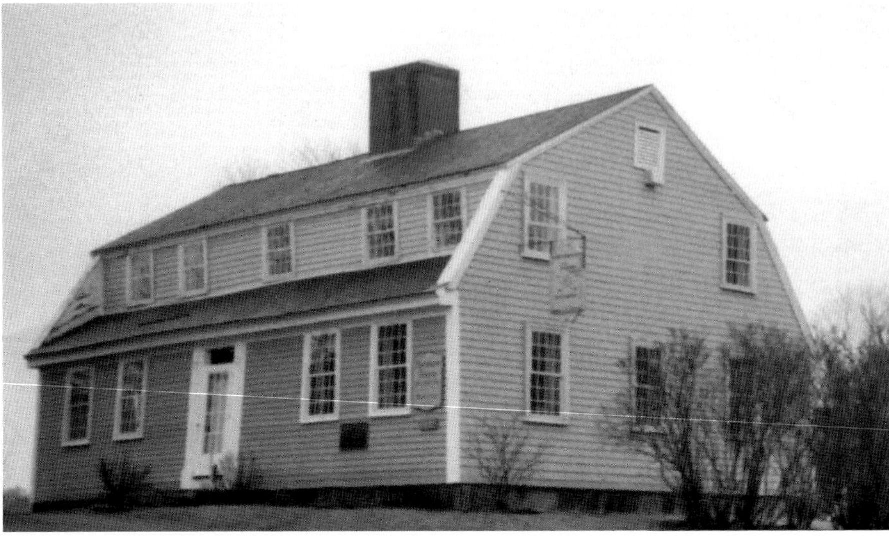

The Burnham Tavern was built in 1770 and today is a historical museum. In 1775, the tavern's taproom was where the decision was made to oppose British forces. *Courtesy of the Burnham Tavern Museum, Machias, Maine.*

the first rebel to be hung in Cumberland County would probably have been Samuel Thompson."

As a post-script to Thompson's War, *Canceaux*'s log contains a letter from Admiral Graves to Andrew Barkley, captain of the frigate HMS *Scarborough* moored in Portsmouth. The letter was dated May 25, 1775. It is important because it reveals Graves's opinion of Mowat's actions at Falmouth.

> *I very much approve and commend Lieutenant Henry Mowat's intrepid and officer like conduct at Falmouth; the behavior of Mr. Hogg also deserves great commendations. It ought to be a caution to all officers not to trust themselves in the hands of rebels, who carry on war like no other people upon earth.*

A month and a half after the dismantling of Fort Pownall, and three weeks after his kidnapping by Samuel Thompson, Captain Mowat and his ship *Canceaux* were still anchored in the Piscataqua River between Portsmouth, New Hampshire, and Kittery.

In the log entry of May 31, 1775, Mowat described, "A great number of armed men, in the amount of five or six hundred, appearing on the shore." (Apparently they were planning to seize some cannon before the British could remove them.) The next day, *Canceaux* was in the company of HMS *Scarborough* when Mowat described an exchange of gunfire with shore batteries. A couple of smaller craft were damaged, and two British sailors were wounded, though the threat subsided when the two warships returned fire.

Canceaux was then ordered to Halifax, Nova Scotia, for a careening (cleaning of the hull), where it spent most of June and July. By early August, the ship was back in Boston Harbor, ready to respond to increasing attempts by Americans to disrupt British maritime operations.

THE MACHIAS AFFAIR

The battle of Machias occurred while *Canceaux* was at Halifax, and Henry Mowat was not involved. The event, however, bears inclusion in our story. It was another step in the worsening relationship between the British authorities and the American Revolutionaries in Maine to which Mowat was so closely and frequently connected. As already mentioned, Admiral Graves would order Mowat to avenge the British naval defeat that resulted by directing him to burn Falmouth.

The Machias Affair was important for several reasons, not the least of which was that it represented a triumph, albeit a small one, by the Americans over a British naval force. Secondly, when news of Thompson's unsuccessful attempt to capture *Canceaux* reached Machias a few weeks later, the example encouraged their militiamen to seize the British schooner *Margaretta* when it arrived in Machias harbor. (They hoped to succeed where Thompson had failed.) Finally, the British defeat at Machias led to the decision by increasingly beleaguered British admiral Samuel Graves to punish townships along the New England coast for their hostile actions toward the Crown. Graves felt he had the perfect man to carry out his plan in Henry Mowat, who was still smarting from his kidnapping by Samuel Thompson.

Machias is in the far corner of down east Maine, twenty-five miles from the Canadian border. The town was settled in 1763, and its eighty odd families were scratching out a meager living by exporting lumber and subsistence farming. When news of the Battles of Lexington and Concord arrived, the patriotic townspeople voted not to provide timber for the British war effort despite the food shortages that their boycott would create.

Not all the people in Maine were anti-British. One was Ichabod Jones, a Tory merchant from Boston, who had been living in Machias for a year. When the crafty trader saw how desperate the town was for food, he decided to take advantage of the Port Act that had closed Boston to colonial traders.

Jones told British officials of his plan. He would provide the timber that the British needed in Boston to build barracks and masts for ships, in exchange for provisions for Machias. Because he was a loyal supporter of the Crown, his proposal was accepted, and he was given permission to pass through the blockade.

Jones was no fool, however, and he requested that an escort ship accompany the two supply vessels he planned to sail to Machias. A small British warship, the armed sloop *Margaretta*, sailed into Machias Harbor on June 2, 1775, under the command of James Moore. *Margaretta* was not heavily armed, but the British commander figured its fourteen swivel guns (small cannons) would be enough to intimidate the local patriots.

Jones proceeded to escalate the situation when he declared that he would only sell food to citizens who agreed to sell him lumber. Angry townspeople gathered in the Burnham Tavern and refused to be bullied by his threats.

The following day was Sunday, and a group of armed men attempted to capture Jones and *Margaretta*'s captain, James Moore, while whey were in church. The two men managed to escape, Jones to the woods and Moore to *Margaretta*. Frustrated in their efforts to stop Moore, a group of men led by Jeremiah O'Brien boarded *Unity*, one of the merchant ships that was at the town dock, and removed the supplies. Another group rowed out to the other supply ship, *Polly*, and attempted to tow it to shore, but it ran aground in the low tide. James Moore, meanwhile, had sailed *Margaretta* downstream, where he anchored for the night to await further developments.

The next day, a group of determined Machias citizens boarded the captured sloop *Unity*. They were armed with a motley collection of weapons, including old muskets, swords, pitchforks and axes. A local schooner, *Falmouth Packet*, was also commandeered, and the little fleet sailed downstream in search of *Margaretta*.

The battle of Machias took place on the morning of June 12, 1775, in Machias Bay. After an exchange of gunfire, men from *Unity* boarded *Margaretta* on one side while *Falmouth Packet* pulled up on the other side. The British sailors fought bravely, but they were outnumbered by the Americans,

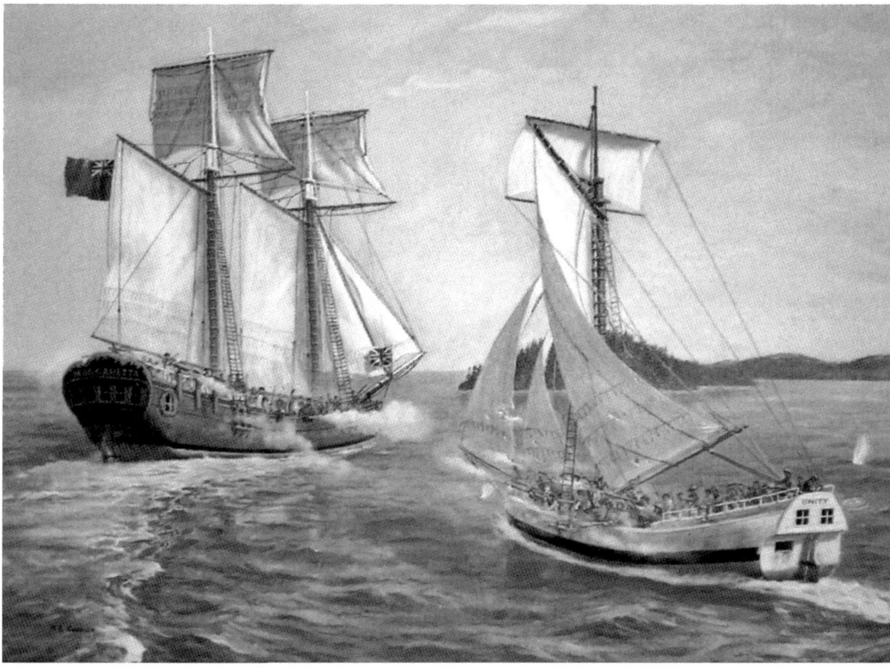

The battle of Machias in 1775 was between the British sloop *Margaretta*, on the left, and the American vessel *Unity*, on the right. This was the first naval engagement in the American Revolution and resulted in an American victory. *Painting by Robert Goodier. It hangs in the Machias Savings Bank in Machias, ME.*

who had an advantage in the hand-to-hand combat that followed. The battle was over in less than an hour.

The jubilant Americans transferred the guns from *Margaretta* to *Polly*, which they named *Machias Liberty*. The British armed schooner *Diligence* was later captured, increasing the size of the American flotilla to four vessels. Thus the "Lexington and Concord of the Sea," as it was called, ended in an American victory. For Admiral Graves, the loss of twenty seamen, including the death of Moore, was a serious blow, much more than the loss of an insignificant schooner. During the following year, the little Maine fleet, under the leadership of Jeremiah O'Brien, patrolled the Maine coast, frequently intercepting merchant ships that were supplying the British army in Boston.

It should be no surprise that British admiral Graves was furious when he heard the results of the battle of Machias. His immediate reaction was to order Henry Mowat to burn Falmouth, which he would do in October 1775. (This action will be fully discussed in the next chapter.)

In August 1777, the British made another attempt to "proceed and reduce Machias," and the attack was again repulsed. One British officer, presumed to be Admiral Graves, supposedly said, "The damned rebels at Machias were a harder set than those at Bunker Hill."

Chapter 4

The Burning of Falmouth

You are to Bestow Your Whole Attention to Annoying the Rebels.
—Samuel Graves's orders to Henry Mowat

Vice admiral Samuel Graves was sixty-one years old when he was appointed commander of the British North American Squadron in 1774. From the beginning of his tenure, the elderly Graves—a favorite of first lord of the admiralty, Lord Sandwich—was clearly in over his head trying to control the explosive situation that had been developing in America over the past decade. By the spring of 1775, the "Surly Old Admiral," as he was called behind his back, was seething. Hostilities at Lexington and Concord, which forced British regulars to retreat to Boston before "a gang of rebels," were the beginning of a series of events that would culminate in Graves ordering Captain Mowat to "pacify" the New England coast in October 1775.

When British General Gage was recalled to report on the outbreak of hostilities around Boston in the spring of 1775, Admiral Graves undoubtedly breathed a sigh of relief, since it was known the two had been feuding for months over how to handle the situation. Graves's feeling was that the gentlemanly, diplomatic Gage had not been aggressive enough in defending Boston. Graves hoped that Gage's replacement, General William Howe, would be a more forceful commander.

Samuel Graves spent most of the summer of 1775 waiting for orders from the admiralty while the situation continued to deteriorate along the New

England coast. Smuggling was rampant as American privateers regularly intercepted British supply ships. In fairness to Graves, the beleaguered vice admiral had only twenty-nine warships to patrol the 1,800-mile coast from Nova Scotia to Florida. The defeat of the British sloop *Margaretta* by rebel ships at Machias in June 1775 and the ongoing refusal of local merchants to provide food for British ships were particularly galling. By the end of the summer, Admiral Graves was virtually imprisoned in Boston Harbor aboard his flagship HMS *Preston*.

Perhaps the last straw was the taking of a British supply vessel carrying a supply of candles. This sent Graves over the edge. (His wife reported he had a fit.) Candles were a seemingly minor item until one considers that they were the only source of light below deck.

In late August, the frustrated Graves took the initiative and ordered his thinly stretched fleet to capture or sink any privateers they encountered. His captains were instructed to "lay waste and destroy every town or place from whence Pirates are fitted out." Not only did these coastal towns shelter rebel privateers, they also supplied them with provisions and replacement gear for their ships. Graves had finally abandoned his "semi-neutrality" in favor of a more aggressive role for the Royal Navy.

When, at last, the sloop of war *Raven* arrived from London on October 4 bringing a packet of letters, Graves's action seemed justified. Included was a dispatch from the admiralty. His orders were as follows:

> *You are required and directed to carry on such operations upon the sea coasts of the Four Governments* [colonies] *in New England, as you shall judge most effectual for suppressing, in conjunction with his Majesty's Land Forces, the Rebellion which is now openly avowed and supported in those colonies.*

The orders brought by *Raven* left Graves a good deal of discretion as to how to implement the directives. This was the situation when Graves turned to his most experienced officer, forty-one-year-old Lieutenant Henry Mowat, to carry out his orders. Graves knew Mowat well. As has been stated, Mowat was chosen because of his detailed knowledge of New England waters, stemming from the *Atlantic Neptune* survey as well as from his connections with many of the people who lived along the coast.

Graves also hoped that by sending Mowat to harass rebel towns, it would keep local militiaman at home. Even more importantly, as George Daughan writes in his book *If By Sea: The Forging of the American Navy*, it would keep patriots from fitting out hundreds of privateers to attack British shipping.

It took several weeks for Mowat to prepare a four-ship squadron of three warships and an armed transport, so he did not sail from Boston until October 13. In an attempt to keep the operation a secret, Graves ordered the stores for the flotilla to be loaded quietly at night.

It was impossible, however, to avoid detection. For example, Timothy Newell, an American soldier, noted in his diary on October 3, "This morning two bomb ketches and several armed vessels with some soldiers are preparing to leave on a secret expedition." Mowat's departure was also noted in the diaries of officers and soldiers at Cambridge, one of whom described the departure of a "strange expedition." A number of them guessed that one destination was Portsmouth. When he was told of the "secret" departure, George Washington was said to have thought the fleet was "bound for New Hampshire or possibly Quebec."

Admiral Graves gave Mowat a four-page list of instructions, which essentially told him to proceed along the coast "to lay waste, burn and destroy such seaport towns as are accessible to his Majesty's ships." Specifically, Mowat was directed to "chastise" the towns of Marblehead, Salem, Newburyport, Cape Ann, Ipswich, Portsmouth, Saco, Falmouth and Machias.

Graves was particularly anxious that the towns of Cape Ann, and distant Machias, be severely punished, since they had recently been the scenes of embarrassing incidents involving the British navy. The Machias defeat, described in the last chapter, was an initial black eye for the British navy. More recently at Cape Ann, the British ship *Falcon* had been seized and her captain and crew imprisoned.

Captain Mowat was reminded not to risk the lives of his men by attempting to occupy the towns and that he should attempt to "differentiate, where possible, between loyalists and rebels, protecting and defending the former while punishing the latter." Mowat was also directed under no circumstances to allow plundering of any sort.

Mowat's fleet sailed on October 8. Many historians feel that considering the modest size of his squadron, his order to attack nine coastal towns with a fleet of three warships and an armed transport was absurd. As a result, the thinking went, he was forced to ignore his orders and concentrate on just one of the proposed targets. Not surprisingly, he would logically select Falmouth, a town he knew well from his run-in with Colonel Samuel Thompson in May 1775.

After the Thompson's War incident, one might assume Mowat was delighted to "chastise" Portland. To commemorate the bicentennial of the event, in 1975, Donald Yerxa wrote *The Burning of Falmouth, A Case Study in British Imperial Pacification*. In his book, Yerxa presents a different explanation for the attack. He states that Mowat's course of action was determined by the weather. Yerxa tells us that Mowat's squadron encountered stormy conditions during its first few days at sea, which delayed his arrival at his first objective, Cape Ann.

On October 11, Mowat maneuvered his vessels close to shore, but on the advice of his artillery officer, Lieutenant Grant, he did not launch an attack because the buildings along Cape Ann were too widely scattered for an effective naval bombardment. Yerxa points out that "Mowat was eager to make a smart showing on his first attempt and equally anxious not to provide the provincials with further encouragement that an unsuccessful bombardment would provide."

Yerxa continued, "The next morning a strong northwest wind carried the flotilla past Newburyport, Ipswich, Portsmouth and Saco to a point off Cape Elizabeth, just south of Falmouth in Casco Bay." Although the winds were strong, there might have been another reason why Mowat decided to bypass Portsmouth.

Colonel Stephen Kemble, deputy adjutant to the British forces, wrote in his journal that Mowat might have stopped at Portsmouth "on his expedition to annoy the coast." However, he was again advised by Lieutenant Grant not to attempt an attack because there was a boom with a strong chain that had been stretched across the entrance to the harbor. The only way a ship could get through was if the boom was raised or lowered by a windlass. Mowat accepted Grant's advice that "such a device offered sufficient reason for not attempting an entrance."

Kemble added, "All the vessels from Cape Ann had fled from Mowat's fleet and were anchored in the Newbury River. The entrance was protected by stakes driven into the bottom." Each of these examples support the point that word of Mowat's expedition had leaked out ahead of time, giving coastal towns time to prepare.

Once Mowat's fleet reached Falmouth, stormy weather drove the expedition north to Boothbay Harbor, where they remained for three days. For the moment, it appeared the squadron was headed for Machias, but a wind shift blocked further passage down east. As a result, on October 16, Mowat left Boothbay Harbor and sailed south to nearby Falmouth Neck.

The Burning of Falmouth

A Horrible Shower of Cannonballs

The stage was now set for the defining event of Henry Mowat's career. Mowat knew Falmouth well, having stopped many times during the *Atlantic Neptune* survey expeditions with surveyors Joseph Des Barres and Samuel Holland. More recently, he had become friendly with the town's moderate leaders, Jedediah Preble and Enoch Freeman, who had helped obtain his release from the fanatical patriot Colonel Thompson the previous spring.

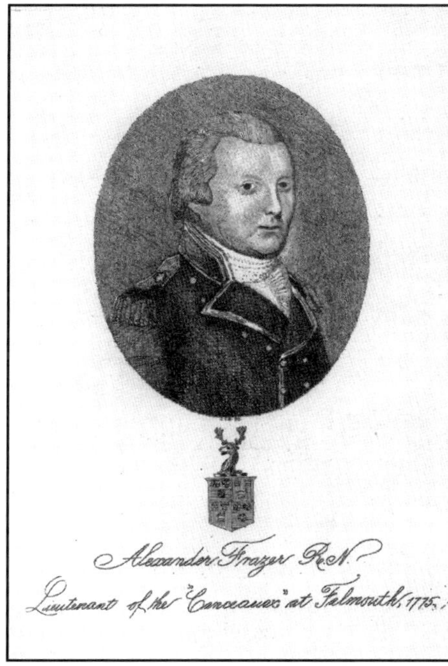

Lieutenant Alexander Fraser was second in command of Mowat's ship, *Canceaux*, anchored in Falmouth harbor. *Courtesy of the Maine Historical Society.*

When three British warships and a transport arrived in Casco Bay on October 16, there was some cause for alarm. This quickly subsided when it was discovered that the commander was the well-known Henry Mowat. Townspeople reassured themselves the British captain intended no harm since they had saved him from the clutches of Samuel Thompson the previous spring.

The next day, October 17, Mowat's second in command, Lieutenant Alexander Fraser, went ashore. Once there, followed by a curious crowd, he proceeded to the town's meetinghouse. On the building's steps, he read the following announcement, a portion of which follows:

> *After so many premeditated attacks on the representatives of the best of sovereigns…you have been guilty of the most unpardonable rebellion supported by the ambitions of a set of designing men…* [My] *orders are to execute a just punishment on the Town of Falmouth. I warn you to remove without delay the human species of said town for which purpose I give you two hours.*

Mowat's proclamation stated that after two hours he would post a red flag on *Canceaux*'s masthead, which would signal the start of "a just punishment."

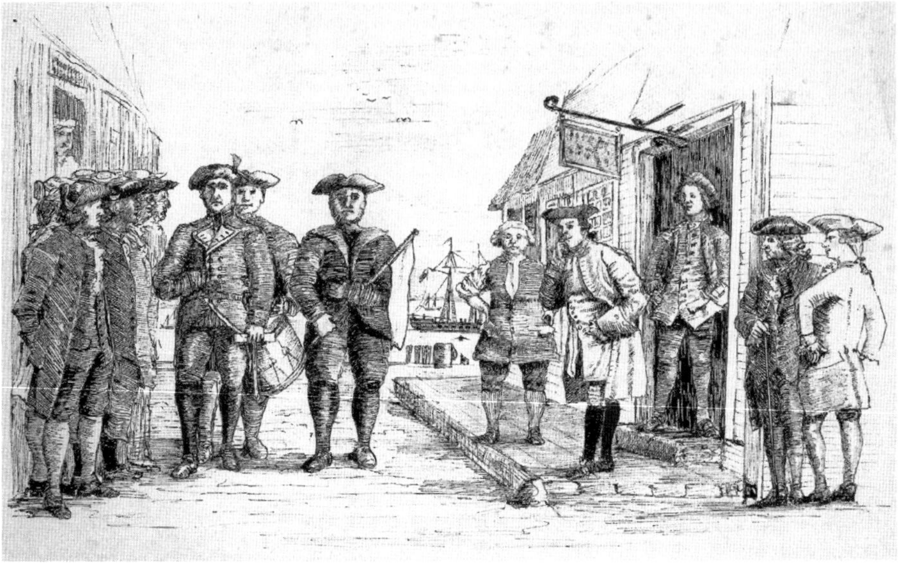

Lieutenant Fraser, accompanied by an armed guard, is shown bringing the fateful announcement from Henry Mowat that he is going to burn the town of Falmouth. *Courtesy of the Maine Historical Society.*

He warned that he would tolerate no "imprudence" and that he expected Lieutenant Fraser to return to the ship "unmolested."

The people of Falmouth were shocked. Reverend Jacob Bailey, a Loyalist and a supporter of the king, wrote, "A frightful consternation ran through the assembly, every heart was seized with terror, every countenance changed color and a profound silence ensued for several moments." Observing the crowd's stunned reaction, Fraser stated he would be willing to carry any messages back to Mowat.

An ad hoc committee of three of Falmouth's moderate citizens—General Jedediah Preble, Dr. Nathaniel Coffin and a merchant, Robert Pagan—rowed out to meet with Mowat to negotiate. On board *Canceaux*, General Preble inquired what exactly was "a just punishment?" Mowat informed him that his orders were to "burn, sink and destroy" Falmouth. Mowat then told Dr. Coffin that he "risked his commission, since his orders from Admiral Graves did not give him the right to negotiate or give any warning to the town before carrying out the 'just punishment.'"

In response to the pleas of the three men, Mowat then departed from his orders and told them that he would not fire on the town if the residents surrendered all their arms by nine o'clock the next morning. "Deliver me five pieces of cannon, your small arms and ammunition, by tomorrow morning

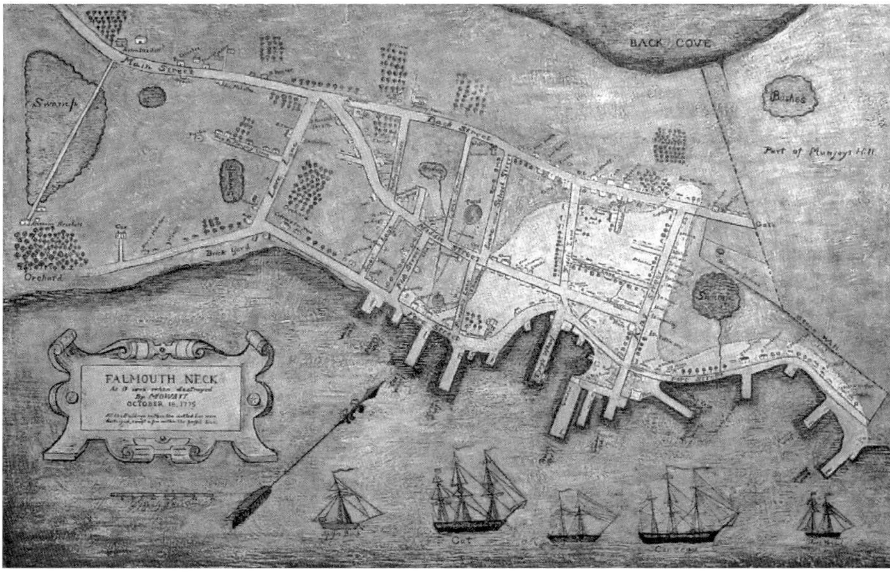

The town of Falmouth Neck was a seaport of two thousand people before it was destroyed by fire. Munjoy Hill, seen on the right of the picture, is where Mowat was apprehended by Samuel Thompson. *Courtesy of the Maine Historical Society.*

and you are safe 'til I hear further from the Admiral, who may be induced to save your town." Here was an olive branch worth considering since it would give Falmouth's inhabitants time to evacuate if a bombardment were to occur.

James Leamon described what happened in Falmouth that night in his book *Revolution Downeast: The War For American Independence in Maine*:

> *During the night, Falmouth was the scene of vast confusion. Residents, convinced that the town would be destroyed, desperately tried to save their possessions; however, there were not enough carts, wagons, wheelbarrows, horses, oxen or hours in the night. By morning, refugees and their belongings still jammed the streets. Adding to the confusion, militia from nearby towns began filtering into Falmouth…In so chaotic an atmosphere the town never did hold its scheduled meeting to consider Mowat's offer* [to turn in all arms and ammunition].

It should be emphasized that, although there was no general town meeting to discuss Mowat's terms, the ad hoc committee simply decided not to surrender Falmouth's arms and ammunition. The committeemen did make one final attempt to dissuade Mowat early the next morning when they rowed out to *Canceaux*. Mowat quickly saw through their delaying tactics and gave them half an hour to get off his ship and clear the town.

The community threatened with destruction by Mowat's flotilla in 1775 was a flourishing commercial town located at the end of a peninsula that jutted several miles out into Casco Bay. Most of the two thousand inhabitants were involved in various maritime enterprises, lumbering or shipbuilding. (Before the Revolution, most of the Province of Maine's timber was exported through Falmouth.)

Falmouth was down east New England's most important seaport and the largest town between Boston and Halifax. The community was well known to British authorities for another reason as well. It was second only to Boston as a center of fierce opposition to the oppressive taxes issued by the British government that had begun with the Stamp Tax in 1766.

That year, Falmouth mobs had attacked unpopular customs officials and supported the citizens of Boston in their opposition to the hated tea tax. Furthermore, they had threatened the British brig *Gaspee* with destruction if its captain attempted to recapture sailors who had deserted in Falmouth. Finally, of course, Thompson's War in the spring of 1775 had simply magnified Falmouth's reputation as a rebel stronghold.

At 9:00 a.m. on the morning of October 18, Captain Mowat scanned the shoreline through his telescope and saw that there were still women and children running around. He therefore waited another forty-five minutes until he was satisfied the waterfront was evacuated.

Finally he gave the order to open fire at 9:45 a.m. Looking back on his damaged career, Mowat would later admit it was an order he performed, "not without reluctance." The first salvo was deliberately aimed high, intended as a final warning to anyone left in the streets or buildings. The first house to be hit belonged to Benjamin Bailey on Middle and Federal Streets. The next, at India and Federal Streets, belonged to Captain Houle. The cannonading would eventually destroy St. Paul's Church, the new courthouse, the public library and the firehouse and fire engine.

In *Curwen's Journal*, on December 19, 1775, it was recorded, "One hundred and thirty nine dwelling houses, two hundred and seventy eight stores and warehouses together and a great number of stables and outbuildings were burnt by Captain Mowat." During the bombardment, buildings worth an estimated £150,000 were destroyed.

Donald Yerxa tells us that for the first few hours the bombardment had little effect on the town because of the poor quality of British ammunition

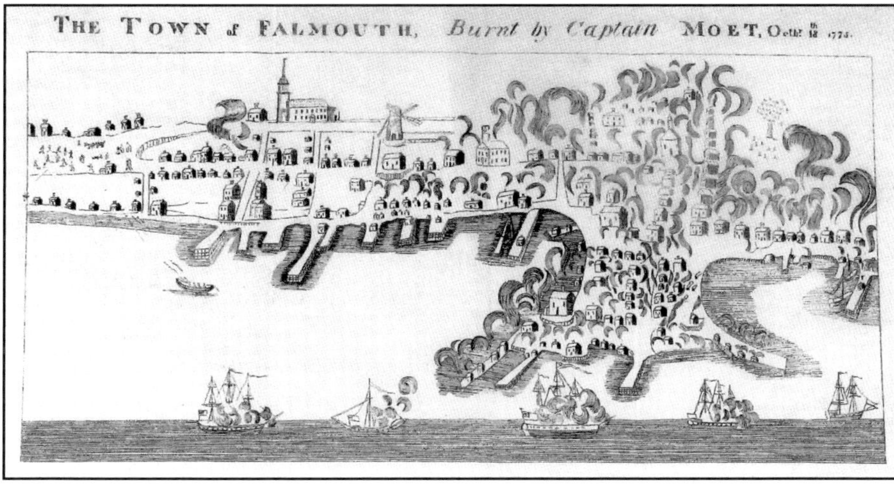

Henry Mowat sent sailors ashore to burn Falmouth after the bombardment from British ships failed to destroy the town. *Courtesy of the Maine Historical Society.*

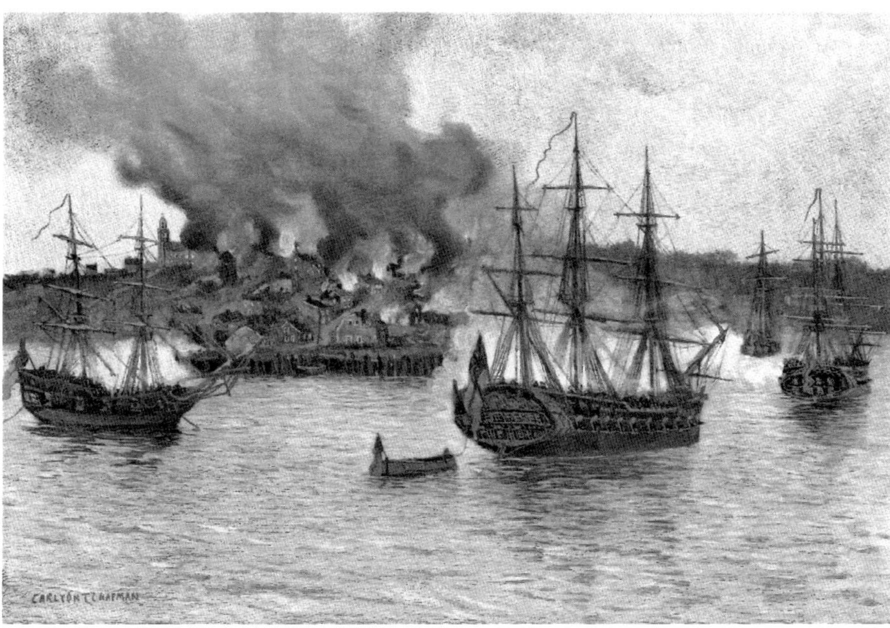

A present-day woodcut of the bombardment of Falmouth. Remarkably, no one on either side was killed. *Courtesy of the North Wind Picture Archives.*

and the stiff breeze that was blowing away from the town. A number of courageous residents of Falmouth also risked their lives running around extinguishing the few fires that had started. The warships continued to bombard the town until mid-afternoon when Mowat realized it would be necessary to send landing parties ashore to complete the job.

Thirty seamen and marines were sent ashore under the command of Lieutenant Fraser at 3:00 p.m. For the next hour, they set fire to many more structures by throwing torches through the doors and windows of houses and stores. A number of colonial militia appeared to oppose them, and there was an exchange of gunfire in which several men on each side were wounded. Yerxa suggests that the militia's arrival probably saved 20 to 30 percent of the town's buildings. He added that, had there been a more organized resistance, much of the town could have been saved, but Falmouth lacked sufficient powder and artillery.

By the end of the afternoon, the actions of the landing party, combined with a shift in the wind, caused a general conflagration. Mowat wrote in his report to Admiral Graves, "Falmouth, with the Blockhouse and battery, the principal wharfs and storehouses was all laid in ashes." The result was that three-quarters of the town was destroyed. In the harbor, there were thirteen vessels that were at anchor when the British arrived. Mowat caught two as they tried to escape and confiscated their cargos. The rest were destroyed by cannon fire.

It is interesting that one result of the landing party was that Mowat lost several men to desertion. In a letter to George Washington describing the attack on Falmouth, Reuben Fogg describes how John Armstrong, a leader of the landing party, voluntarily surrendered himself to colonial militia and said "he chose to fight for America." Fogg continued, "I now send him to your headquarters to be examined by your Excellency."

After leaving Yarmouth, three more seamen deserted when the fleet anchored farther up the coast at North Yarmouth. All three had been impressed into the navy and seized the first opportunity to flee.

During the bombardment of Falmouth, Mowat's four ships had fired an estimated three thousand rounds of shot at Falmouth. There were a few injuries, although remarkably no one was killed on either side. The bombardment, however, took its toll on Mowat's ships. *Canceaux* was originally constructed as a merchant ship, and its hull was never designed to absorb the jarring effects of eight hours of cannon fire. Planks began to open up and it was necessary to keep the pumps operating continuously for the elderly survey ship to remain afloat.

Canceaux's log referred to another member of the squadron, the sloop *Spitfire*, "as being much shattered and in need of repair." Indeed, *Spitfire*'s hull had sustained so much damage from the firing of its guns that Mowat was concerned about its ability to make the return trip to Boston.

The log also recorded other problems. Mowat wrote, "The troops are also in great distress for want of necessary [essentials]. Many of them embarked without a second shirt, from which cause they are rendered incapable of their duty, and are falling sick very fast." The master of *Halifax* would die of small pox a few weeks later, and the ship's crew was quarantined in Boston Harbor for weeks.

Under the circumstances, Mowat decided to cancel the rest of his raid along the coast and return to Boston. He had expended all of his ammunition, and his ships were literally coming apart at the seams. Certainly they were in no condition to attack the remaining towns on the list Admiral Graves had given him.

The squadron remained in the Casco Bay area for the next six days while temporary repairs were made on the ships. Meanwhile, *Canceaux*'s log reported, "On shore the fires were still continuous in town." The little fleet finally headed south on October 25 and reached their mooring at Nantasket Road (anchorage) on the edge of Boston Harbor on November 2.

George Daughan wrote in *If by Sea*:

> *The most Mowat could do was to limp back to port, relieved that no storm or patriot warships were around to threaten his hobbled squadron. In the end, rather than demonstrating the strength of the Royal Navy, the burning of Falmouth actually revealed its limitations. Nor did it succeed in cowing the patriots. It only served to enrage the country and strengthen the rebellion.*

SOME EYEWITNESS ACCOUNTS

The Reverend Jacob Bailey's letter described the sequence of events from the time Mowat's fleet was sighted passing Falmouth until after the bombardment. Portions are included:

> *On Friday the 13th of October, the inhabitants were alarmed by the appearance of a fleet, which passed the harbor and stretched along the*

> *eastern shores. The wind was blowing in heavy squalls from the northwest.* [This was why the fleet ended up at Boothbay.]
>
> *On Sunday a report prevailed in town that the fleet had taken a number of sheep from a neighboring island and that as a consequence of some opposition one or two buildings were consumed by fire. These reports induced the people to conclude that the design of the expedition was only to procure provisions for the* [British] *forces in Boston who were now represented in starving condition.*
>
> *In a few minutes the whole town* [Falmouth] *was involved in smoke and combustion…The bombardment continued from half after nine till sunset, during which all the lower and middle of the town was reduced to a heap of rubbish…The front of the Meeting-house was torn to pieces by the bursting of a bomb. In a word, about three quarters of the town was consumed and between two and three hundred families who, twenty-four hours before enjoyed tranquility, were now destitute.*

The Reverend Samuel Dean's letter to Benjamin Greenleaf, November 4, 1775, described the situation:

> *Such is our present dismal situation that unless something is done for us we are absolutely undone…About two thirds of the buildings, in general the best, have been laid in ashes…Another affair I would entreat you to take into consideration is the lamentable state of the poor of Falmouth who have lost their habitations and many of their movables…If the war continues six months longer, this shall probably involve the whole province of Maine in our ruin.*

Daniel Tucker was fifteen at the time of Mowat's attack and wrote:

> *He* [Mowat] *returned again in October with five vessels under his command. They arrived and anchored in the lower harbor on the 16th without any communication with the town and the inhabitants were greatly terrified at the appearance of this hostile force until it was ascertained that Captain Mowat was in command…My master Paul Little came to the shop and told me that if Captain Mowat had the command there was no danger.*
>
> *…An officer came ashore under a flag of truce and stated he had orders to set the town on fire immediately. A respectable committee went on board the* Canceaux *and entered into conference with Mowat and*

with much difficulty persuaded him to defer his work of destruction until morning.

...When I heard the town was to be burned I took all the money out of the shop. With nobody to help me but the females, I got everything ready to load up in carts until my master arrived.

...The first shot whistled between me and the old meeting house. The other vessels then commenced their spiteful fire and continued with very little cessation until six o'clock, PM...Many people have blamed the inhabitants of Falmouth for not defending the town but the truth is there was not a cannon mounted in town and there was a great scarcity of power.

Stephen Kemble from York, Maine, wrote in his journal:

Mr. Mowat arrived this day from his expedition to annoy the coast, and says that on Wednesday 18th of October he burned Falmouth. General Preble first came on board not believing it was intended to destroy the place, but when assured of it returned on shore to apprise the inhabitants.

...General Preble assured Mowat that he had taken no part in the Rebellion. That he had been offered a Command in the Provincial Troop, but did not accept it.

Recollections of Mrs. Nathaniel Wilson, age 102:

The man who was sent on shore by Captain Mowat to set fire to the first parish-meeting house in Portland was brought to her house as a prisoner on his way to Boston. [Presumably this was John Armstrong.] *She thinks that if the Committee of Safety had followed the advice of Colonel Thompson, who had made a prisoner of Captain Mowat when he was on shore on a gunning excursion, the town would not have been destroyed.*

MOWAT'S ACTIONS EVALUATED

How are we to judge Henry Mowat's actions from the time he received his orders from Admiral Graves to "make the most vigorous efforts to burn the towns and destroy the shipping in the harbors of coastal Massachusetts and the Province of Maine?"

Captain Mowat intended to begin his cruise with the bombardment of Cape Ann until his artillery officer persuaded him it was not the best place to launch an initial attack on coastal towns. His little fleet was then swept past other towns on the list by strong winds. By the time the storm subsided, he was beyond Falmouth and had to sail back to Casco Bay.

Once his ships arrived in Falmouth Harbor, Mowat sent Lieutenant Alexander Fraser ashore to announce his intentions to destroy the town in two hours. Seeing the crowd's reaction, Mowat wrote that "Fraser was persuaded to allow a number of the principled people who had never joined in the rebellion" to come on board *Canceaux* to meet with Mowat. The negotiations that ensued have been described, and we know that Mowat allowed himself to be convinced to delay his attack until the following morning.

When he returned to Boston, Mowat sent a fourteen-page report to Admiral Graves describing the expedition. Regarding his decision to postpone the attack, he wrote, "The known humanity of the British Nation encouraged me to take this action." Indeed, he reminded Graves that he was simply following orders by attempting to distinguish between the rebels and the Loyalist residents of Falmouth. That was why he allowed the ad hoc committee of Preble, Coffin and Pagan to meet with him aboard *Canceaux*.

Mowat's report also stated that the next morning he delayed his attack for an additional forty-five minutes when he saw women and children remaining on the shoreline. We need not further describe the details of the shelling that ensued except to say that by mid-afternoon Mowat realized he would need to send a party ashore to complete the job.

At the conclusion of his report, Mowat informed Admiral Graves that they had "great difficulty in accomplishing this piece of service [bombing the town] as we soon experienced the insufficiency of artillery stores not only in goodness but in quantity." Mowat added that a "want of troops" also prevented him from sweeping through Falmouth to confiscate the arms and ammunition.

In sum, Captain Mowat's report to Graves would appear to be a remarkably candid account of his cruise and one that was largely supported by the eyewitness accounts. When he later came in for criticism, Mowat's defense naturally would be that he was "following orders." By carrying out these orders, however, his name would be tarnished as a part of Maine's history for the next two hundred years.

Although Admiral Graves was pleased that Falmouth had been largely destroyed, he felt that Captain Mowat had only partially followed his instructions, since he had destroyed only one of the nine towns on the list that he had been given. In a letter to Philip Stephens, secretary to the admiralty, Graves later expressed his displeasure. Nor was he happy that Mowat had allowed the inhabitants of Falmouth time to evacuate before launching his attack, which had also gone against his orders.

OTHER REACTIONS

The Quaker general Nathaniel Greene was one of George Washington's leading generals throughout the Revolution. Greene was at his home in Prospect Hill, Massachusetts, when he heard Falmouth had been burned. He wrote Washington the following letter on October 24, portions of which are included.

> *I learned last night the greater part of the town is in ashes…No person was killed or wounded during the whole time of the firing…The enemy proceeded under orders from Admiral Graves to burn all towns from Boston to Halifax…Captain Mowat also acquainted the Committee that he expected the City of New York was in ashes. By this outcome we learn what we may have to expect. I think Newport should be fortified in the best manner it can be…Fight on or be slaves is the American motto!*

Greene's letter was important because it confirmed what England's response would be to the rebellion. The harsh attitude toward the colonies started at the top. King George III was incensed that American provincials would have the temerity to oppose him and that they would even consider threatening independence if the Crown did not respond to their pleas for representation.

With the appointment of Lord George Germain in 1775, the die was cast. Germain fully expected that with aggressive military action, and the full might of the Royal Navy, the war would be over in a year. The Continental Congress was currently meeting in Philadelphia waiting for King George to respond to the Olive Branch Petition, which was an appeal to "remain friends." Instead, Congress received the news of Falmouth's destruction the same day that news arrived that the British government was raising an army of German mercenaries to be employed against the American colonies. The effect was devastating.

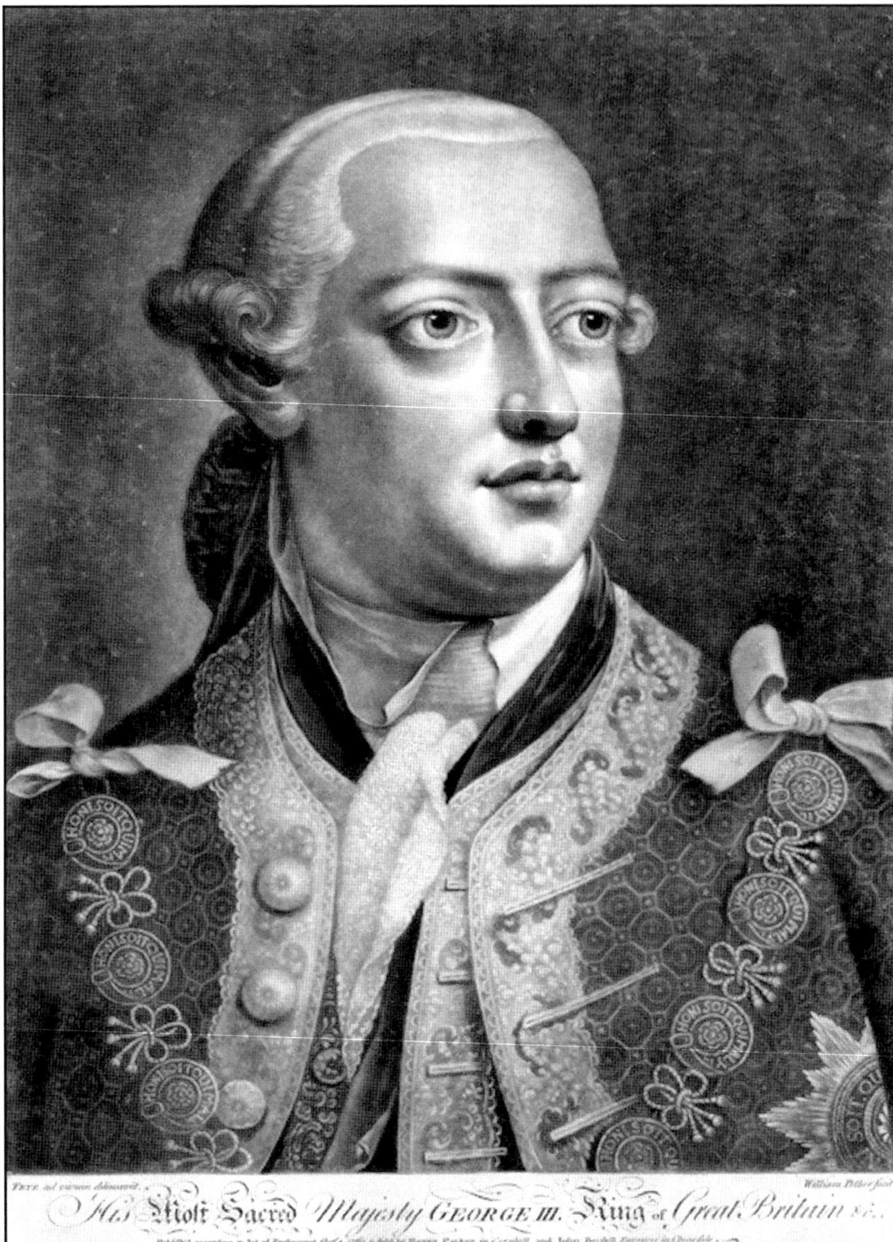

King George III blamed Admiral Graves for ordering Henry Mowat to "lay waste the seaport towns," which fanned the flames of Revolution. *Courtesy of Wikipedia.*

George Washington wrote several letters to the people of Falmouth responding to their pleas for help while at the same time expressing his horror at the event. "The general suffering is beyond the measure of my feelings." His letter written on November 6, 1775, summarizes his concerns as well his inability to do much to alleviate the situation.

> *I have received your letters and am very sorry it is not in my power to supply the necessities of the Town of Falmouth. I have referred the gentleman who brought me your letter to the General Court of the Province who, I hope, will fall upon some method for your assistance…I sincerely sympathize with the people in distress, but in such times they should exert themselves in the noble cause of liberty.*

Mowat's bombardment of a seemingly defenseless town made the headlines throughout America, as well as England and France. In England, opinion was divided. Some newspapers reserved judgment until the event was verified; others expressed regret and considered the assault an affront to justice since the people of Falmouth, although colonials, nevertheless were British citizens. When the French foreign minister Vergennes was informed, his reply was, "Such an action was barbaric as well as a strategic absurdity."

In North America, the episode was widely condemned and quickly became a favorite topic of conversation and correspondence. James Warren wrote to John Adams describing the "pirates on the Eastern Shore as savage and barbarous in the highest stage. What do we wait for now? What more can we want to justify any step to apprehend our enemies, to confiscate their goods and estates, to open our ports to foreigners and form alliances."

George Trevelyan, in his history of the American Revolution, wrote, "The doom of Falmouth was a foretaste of what the Northern colonies could expect." These two pieces of intelligence (the other being the hiring of German mercenaries), by their simultaneous effect, killed all hope, or even desire, of reconciliation. A southern delegate said to his New England colleague, "Brother rebel, I am ready to declare ourselves independent. We have now got a sufficient answer to our petition."

William Barry, archivist at the Maine Historical Society, wrote an article entitled "Portland Fire Starter: Mowat, Monster or Tortured Soul." Commenting on the burning of Falmouth, Barry wrote:

> *Among Americans it strengthened the resolve of rebels and pushed neutrals toward the rebel camp. Indeed, the Declaration of Independence, signed the following summer, had the attack in mind when it charged King George with having "plundered our Seas, ravaged our Coast and burnt our towns."*

It is part of Maine's folklore that parents used the event to discipline unruly children. For years after the Falmouth burning, it is said that disobedient youngsters were threatened by the specter of Captain Mowat coming to punish them.

WHO WAS TO BLAME?

Admiral Graves, upon receiving Mowat's report, was initially pleased with the results. He wrote in his letter to Philip Stephens, secretary to the admiralty, on November 6. "This, however, is a severe stroke to the rebels, Falmouth having long been a principal magazine of all kinds of merchandize."

When the British leadership, including King George, became aware of what Graves had ordered, the admiral was roundly criticized for planning the attack with such limited resources. Apparently, the king was particularly furious. At that point, Graves belatedly attempted to shift the blame to Mowat for disobeying his orders.

Upon hearing what had happened, General William Howe, now commander of British land forces in North America, was also dismayed, believing that only the waterfront areas of the towns in question would be destroyed. George Daughan adds, "Even Lord George Germain, who was fiercely 'anti-American,' found Graves' actions excessive, they seemed a grotesque overcompensation for his pitiful lack of activity in the previous months."

The indignant Germain wrote to Howe, "Why did he [Graves] proceed to that extremity without an absolute refusal on the part of the inhabitants to comply with those requisitions stated in the orders he received from the Lords of the Admiralty?"

Admiral Graves now had to reconcile himself to the fact that his scheme to "lay waste the seaport towns" had failed. The British offensive had stalled, and any further action would have to wait until spring. Under these circumstances, it was probably a blessing that Graves was recalled and replaced by Lord Richard Howe, brother of General William Howe, as commander of the North American Squadron.

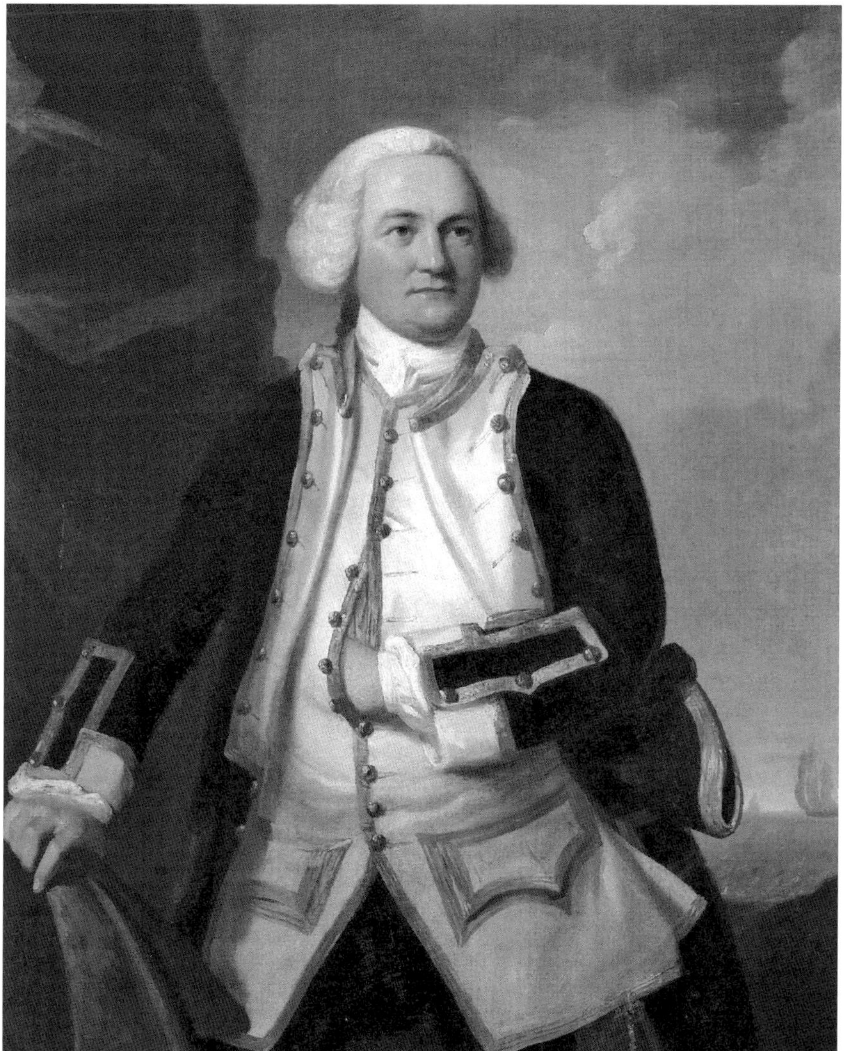

Admiral Samuel Graves commanded the British North American Squadron headquartered in Boston. He was criticized for the turmoil associated with the beginning of the Revolution and was replaced by Admiral Richard Howe (the brother of General William Howe) in January 1776. *Courtesy of Wikipedia.*

Criticism of Graves also came, unexpectedly, from the pen of British general John Burgoyne, currently stationed in America, and whose experience as a playwright had refined his wit. Excerpts follow from a letter he wrote to his friend George Germain:

> *What is the Admiral doing? I wish I was able to answer that question satisfactorily, but I can only say what he is not doing. He is not supplying the troops with sheep and oxen diners. He is not defending his flocks and herds for the enemy has repeatedly, and insultingly plundered his appropriated islands. He is not defending the other islands in the harbor, for the enemy has landed in force. And he is not employing his ships to keep up communication and intelligence.*

James Phinney Baxter was a distinguished historian and mayor of Portland for six years. Baxter represented the views of most nineteenth-century Mainers with the talk he gave at the Maine Historical Society in 1890. "It is sufficient for us to say that Henry Mowat ruthlessly and needlessly destroyed a thriving and well ordered town, peopled with men and women of his own race and scattered them abroad exposed to suffering and death from want, hardship and exposure."

Just a few years later, however, Charles Edward Banks read a paper at the Maine Historical Society in 1894 entitled "The Destruction of Falmouth in 1775 and the Responsibility Therefore." Banks had made an exhaustive study of Henry Mowat's role and reached the conclusion that Mowat had not only been made a scapegoat "but that he was in receipt of the commendation of his superiors, was received in audience by George the Third and got a promotion at that time for services acceptably rendered." (This was an exaggeration, since the promotion was delayed for seven years.)

Roger Duncan wrote in his book *Coastal Maine: A Maritime History*, published in 1992, "In later years both Mowat and Graves suffered for the deed. Graves was relieved of command in December 1775 for having failed to kill wasps with his baseball bat and never held another command."

When he finally returned to England in 1782, Mowat wrote a lengthy statement, "A Relation of the Services in which Captain Henry Mowat of the Royal Navy was Engaged in America from 1759 to the End of the American War in 1783," in which he criticized the admiralty for his lack of advancement stating that his commission as post captain should date from 1776 and not 1782. Not until 1783 did he finally achieve post rank (captain).

Chapter 5

Interlude: 1776 to 1779

In Falmouth, a committee was formed to raise funds for the 160 families, about 1,000 people out of an estimated population of 2,500, who were left homeless. Charitable contributions arrived from nearby towns, although there was a strong feeling among the more rabid patriots in the surrounding counties that Falmouth got what it deserved for its timidity in the face of the enemy. The Massachusetts General Council did authorize £250 to be paid to distressed families and for food to be distributed to those left destitute.

Rebuilding Falmouth was a slow process as long as the Revolution was going on, and many Loyalists and refugees fled the area altogether. By 1784, however, forty homes and ten shops had been constructed, and by 1797, over four hundred homes, factories, offices and public buildings had been built.

HMS *Canceaux* was given a quick refit in Boston before transporting Captain Mowat and a skeleton crew across the stormy Atlantic in January 1776. When it reached the Royal Naval base at Portsmouth, the ship was laid up, presumably for further repairs. One of the last references in *Canceaux*'s log, however, was to "the Commissioner paying the ship's company off." This occurred on April 16, 1776. After twelve years of service in the Royal Navy, it would appear the decrepit old vessel was decommissioned. For the time being, Mowat was left without a ship.

Samuel Graves also returned to England in 1776. The irritable admiral proceeded to get into a heated argument with John Montagu, the fourth earl of Sandwich and first lord of the admiralty, over his next assignment, which he declined to accept. Graves resigned from the navy in a huff and retired to write his memoirs.

Proceeding from Portsmouth to London, Henry Mowat also met with John Montagu, the first sea lord. Given the length and successes of his service in America, he requested command of a frigate. Sandwich put him off, not wanting to reveal that by destroying Falmouth he had angered King George.

With masterful equivocation, Sandwich then replied that he would be pleased to give Mowat a frigate but that "none were ready for Commission," (untrue). Sandwich then ordered Mowat to return to Boston and "take command of a ship lying there recommended as extremely fit for service" (it wasn't). He also insinuated that Mowat might soon be made post captain of the ship (he wasn't). If not, Sandwich implied, "he would be appointed to the first vacant post ship in America" (he wasn't).

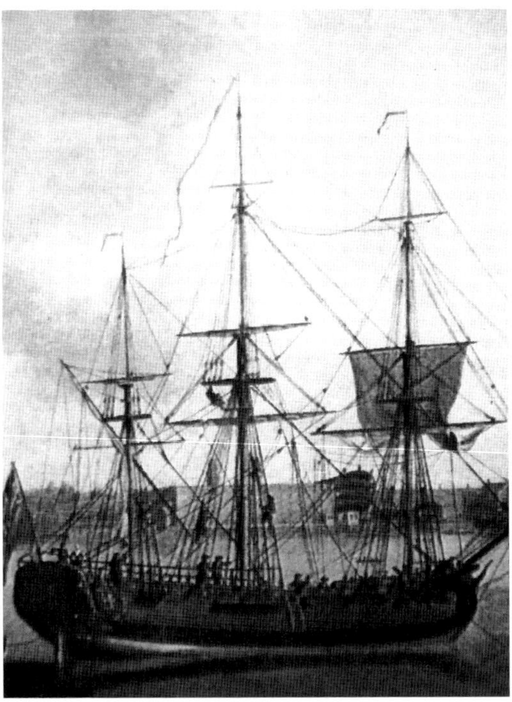

After returning *Canceaux* to England, Henry Mowat was ordered back to Boston where he was given command of the sixteen-gun sloop *Albany*. *Courtesy of John Flint.*

Captain Mowat dutifully returned to Boston, where he was given command of the sixteen-gun sloop *Albany* in June 1776. An item in the Boston *Independent Chronicle* noted that the new commander was "The well known, brutal Henry Mowat who cruelly plundered and burnt Casco Bay."

We know that for the next six years, Mowat was continuously passed over for promotion to post captain and that he grew increasingly frustrated with the situation. He found it particularly galling when his former first lieutenant of marines on *Canceaux*, the very capable Alexander Fraser, was promoted ahead of him. Despite the fact that Fraser was of noble birth, this was considered a gross violation of the seniority list. It wasn't long before Mowat came to the realization that the smooth-talking first lord had deceived him in more ways than one.

By most accounts, Henry Mowat does not appear to have been a vengeful or cruel man. He had been surveying North American waters since 1764, and over the years, he had gained the respect of many of the inhabitants of New England's coastal towns. Mowat could be an agreeable man to those he met, and he had made a number of good friends, some of whom rescued him in Falmouth from Colonel Thompson.

Sources agree that Henry Mowat was probably the most conscientious, knowledgeable and competent officer in the North American Squadron at the start of the Revolution. Admiral Shuldham, who replaced Admiral Graves for a short time before Lord Howe took over the North American Squadron, referred to him as "the most useful person in America under naval authority."

Some contemporary descriptions of Henry Mowat follow.

> *He was the picture of a neat, clear-eyed sea captain with high-arched black eyebrows and a fresh countenance...A haughty, fine looking man in his full naval uniform...A little above middle size and quick to temper...A bit of a dandy and fond of powdering his hair...Dressed in his light blue–faced uniform, he cut a handsome figure as a Royal Navy officer.*

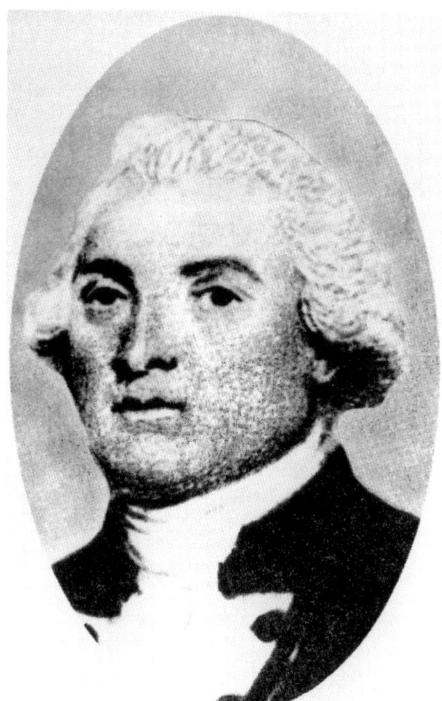

Because of his extensive knowledge of the east coast of North America from his twelve-year survey, Henry Mowat was considered to be "the most useful person in America under naval authority" by the admiralty. *Courtesy of the Maine Historical Society.*

The captain could be a gracious host. During the coastal surveys on *Canceaux* before the Revolution, he would often invite local townspeople aboard his ship. There is an account of a conversation he had with a Portland merchant captain named John Beath who described the following evening:

> *Captain Mowat dipped his colors to my flag and invited me to dine. His manners were courtly and companionable and I found his society agreeable…I observed his iron chest was left with the cover open and a good supply of coins was visible. Gradually the conversation tended to the state of the colonies and Captain Mowat expatiated with enthusiasm on the glory of the British navy.*
>
> *And you Captain, ought to take command under her—the finest frigate in the Royal Navy will be yours if you will give up these uneasy notions and take office under her flag, and he glanced at the open chest of gold and extended his hand cordially.*
>
> *I did not accept the proffered hand nor did I flare up as some do. I was his guest, and I simply shook my head and quietly but firmly said, Captain Mowat I am a poor man but there isn't gold enough in the Bank of England to buy me.*
>
> *After that we tried to talk as usual, but it was no use, the merchant captain continued. We were both of us men of opinions and principles, though widely differing.*

Charles Banks wrote in the *Portland Daily Argus*, January 27, 1912, that "Captain Mowat was a married man." However, Banks was never able to discover whether Mowat's wife, if he had one in the first place, was English or American or when his marriage occurred, though he thinks it occurred before 1775. To add to the confusion, Banks thinks that Mowat might have become a widower by 1775. If true, this would help explain his later relationships with other women.

We do know that Mowat had a daughter and a son, who he states in his will was named William, although there are sources that refer to him as John Alexander. The child was apparently with his father when Colonel Thompson arrested him in Falmouth. Mowat obviously cared for the boy and arranged for his education with Loyalists in Halifax, Nova Scotia, after the Revolution.

Mowat had an eye for pretty ladies. He was reportedly smitten by the lovely eighteen-year-old Mary Sparhawk, the only daughter of the Loyalist

Nathaniel Sparhawk, who lived in Kittery, across the Piscataqua River from Portsmouth, New Hampshire. Much has been written about the many months passed by Captain Henry Mowat while *Canceaux* was moored in Spruce Creek, near the Sparhawk house in Kittery. Nor, apparently, was Mowat deterred when Mary married the elderly Dr. Charles Jarvis in 1773 or 1774. One source suggests that a possible reason Portsmouth was spared from bombardment in 1775 was due to his ongoing "friendship" with Mary.

Mary Sparhawk was not the only woman in Mowat's life. The elegant Mrs. Kenney—"a most beautiful woman in her day," according to a letter written by Elizabeth Oakes Smith—also fascinated him. There is the story that Mrs. Kenney might have been aboard *Canceaux* when Falmouth was bombarded. There seems to be no question that she was a resident of that ill-fated town.

Upon his return to North America in 1776, Henry Mowat shifted his flag to several different ships. After six months on *Albany*, Sir George Collier appointed him acting commander of two other British warships, the first being HMS *Milford*. This was followed by a brief stint on HMS *Scarborough*. Mowat returned to HMS *Albany* in May 1777, a ship he considered an insult to his abilities as a captain.

While he was on patrol as interim commander of the twenty-eight-gun frigate HMS *Milford*, Mowat twice tangled with the legendary American naval captain John Paul Jones. Their encounters in the fall of 1776 are described in a book entitled *A Naval History of the American Revolution*, (date unknown) by a historian identified by the name of Cooper: "Captain Mowat was off the coast of the Carolinas and had a brush with Captain John Paul Jones in the *Providence* of twelve guns." The next month, Cooper describes "the same weasel" chasing Captain Jones in the *Alfred* into Boston Harbor and putting his ship out of action. By now, Mowat was practically considered a war criminal in America, although a London newspaper hailed his cruise as "the most successful of the fall [1777] season."

For the next two years, Mowat made a name for himself as a "fighting captain." In command of *Milford*, he was credited with the destruction of twelve American vessels, including six that he burnt in Boston Harbor. The commander of the Port of Boston, the distinguished Commodore John Manley, was so unnerved by the infamous Captain Mowat lurking off shore that he never sailed out to engage him.

Later that year, while still commanding HMS *Milford*, Mowat forced the American brig *Cabot* ashore on the coast of Nova Scotia, where it was abandoned. Mowat spent the next two weeks refloating the vessel and brought it to Halifax for refitting.

It must have been frustrating for Mowat that, in spite of his numerous triumphs over American ships while commanding *Milford* and *Scarborough*, he was still not promoted to the rank of post captain. Instead, as he later complained, he was forced "to return to the wretched *Albany*," as "Lieutenant in Command" in 1777.

Albany's new commander found his 230-ton sloop to be a minimal improvement over the battered old *Canceaux*. His ship was ninety-one feet long, had a beam of twenty-six feet and carried a crew of 125 men. It was armed with sixteen cannons.

At the start of the American Revolution, the British had bought a number of Boston-built sloops like *Albany*, but their shallow draughts and poor accommodations for officers and crew made them less than appealing to ships' captains. Ironically, Mowat himself had recommended *Albany*'s purchase, although he had not expected to command it.

Winters aboard *Albany* were particularly unpleasant, with northeast gales, blizzards and the pressure of constant patrolling. The coast was still largely uncharted except for sketches that Mowat had personally made on his survey expeditions aboard *Canceaux*. Not surprisingly, there were more than a few encounters with unmarked rocks.

Henry Mowat would command HMS *Albany* for five long years, from 1777 to 1782. The now notorious captain continued to prowl the New England coast, preying on American merchant ships, taking prizes and protecting the sea lanes between New York and Halifax. In reality, most of the time *Albany* guarded Canadian waters from rebel fishermen, an assignment the Scottish captain found demeaning for an officer of his seniority and talents.

Chapter 6

The Expedition to the Penobscot

The British historian W.L. Clowes characterized the Penobscot Expedition as "an enterprise bad in conception, bad in preparation and bad in execution."

The town of Castine was known by its Indian name Majabagaduce, or Bagaduce, in the eighteenth century. The town sits on a spit of land at the northern part of Penobscot Bay near the entrance to the Penobscot River. As the Revolution progressed, the British realized the importance of this strategic location, and in 1779, a decision was made to build a fort and establish a naval base at what was considered to be one of the finest natural harbors on the Atlantic coast.

There were a number of reasons behind the decision. A base at Bagaduce would improve the fraying lines of communication between Halifax, Nova Scotia, and British headquarters in New York. A secure post in Penobscot Bay would be three hundred miles closer to the American-held town of Boston than the present facility at Halifax, which would allow the Royal Navy to strengthen its blockade of New England. Finally, Bagaduce had the advantage of usually being ice-free in the winter.

There were also political advantages to establishing a base in the Penobscot region. Loyalists who had been displaced from their homes in colonies to the south were moving into the area. Building a fort would give them protection while they started new lives. A fort would also allow the British to resettle the numerous Loyalist refugees who had fled to Halifax and were living in miserable, overcrowded conditions. Finally, a

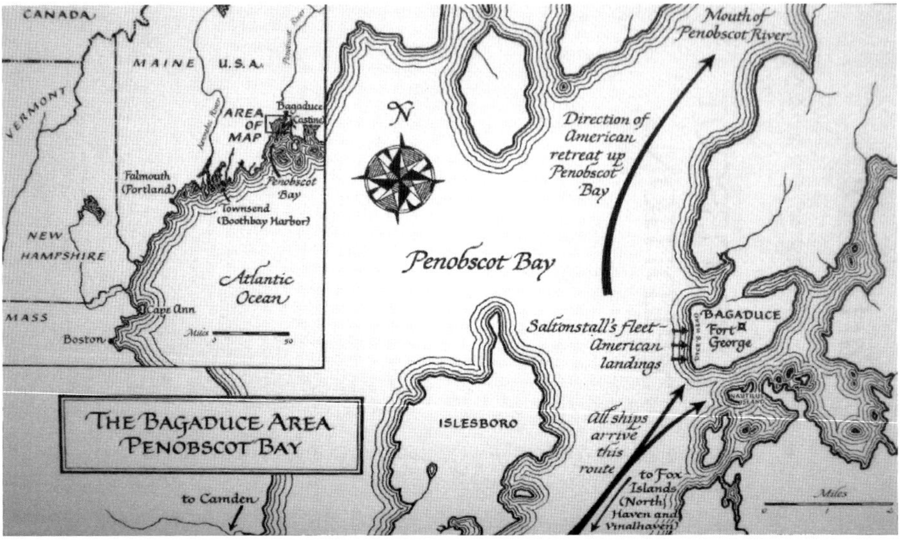

A map showing the northern parts of Penobscot Bay as they relate to events in the Penobscot Expedition. *Courtesy of Charles Bracelen Flood, from his book* Rise and Fight Again.

Loyalist center in Maine would provide a buffer zone for the British in Nova Scotia.

Lastly, before the American Revolution, the forests of Maine were considered ideal timber for the masts of Royal Navy ships. Once the Revolution began, transporting the wood to shipyards at Halifax had become a risky business, since American privateers preyed on the cargo ships. John Cayford wrote in his article "The Ill-Fated Penobscot Expedition," "The entire coast of Maine had become a thorn in the side of the Royal Navy." It was hoped that a fort at Bagaduce would improve British control of the area and reduce the risk of harassment.

The Expedition Is Launched

The Bay of the Penobscot is spacious and capable of containing all the Navies of the World.
—Henry Mowat

Henry Mowat continued to patrol the Maine coast in his sloop of war *Albany* for what seemed like an eternity until he was summoned to Halifax in the winter of 1779. There he was told of a daring British plan to open a new front in the war against their rebellious colonies. Charles B. Flood, in his book *Rise and Fight Again*, wrote, "After four years of fighting the British had been unable to drive a wedge through the colonies. Now they were embarked upon a strategy of chopping off the ends and inland edges of this new entity." In the south, Savannah, Georgia, had been captured and the British hoped to march through the Carolinas to Virginia.

The British scheme in the north was to build a fort at Bagaduce (Castine) at the mouth of the Penobscot River. Admiral Marriot Arbuthnot, commander of the northern station, told Mowat his assignment would be to command a flotilla of warships and convoy two highland regiments from Halifax to the site of the proposed fort at Bagaduce. The destination of the expedition was to be a secret from everyone except the commander of the highland regiments, General Francis McLean.

As has been stated, Henry Mowat was acknowledged as the British officer who knew the coastal waters of Maine better than anyone else in the navy. We can only imagine his reaction to Admiral Arbuthnot's words. He knew the mood of many of the people who lived on the coast and, remembering Colonel Thompson's actions at Falmouth, quickly realized that the independent-minded Yankees of Massachusetts would never tolerate the building of a fort in the middle of the Province of Maine. After four years of war, hostilities were too far advanced for Americans to accept the action without mounting a major retaliatory force.

At the meeting, Henry Mowat boldly protested that the idea was a disaster in the making and strongly advised against the construction of a fort on the Penobscot. He predicted (correctly) that the Americans would attempt to dislodge the operation, which would leave the British forces in Halifax with an insufficient force to repulse a possible attack. (His second prediction was incorrect, since there was never an American attack on Halifax.) In any case, we know that Admiral Arbuthnot brushed aside Mowat's concerns and ordered him to proceed with the expeditionary force.

Being the loyal officer that he was, Mowat accepted his orders, although he considered the mission to be foolhardy. The final straw was that he would have to lead the expedition in the decrepit sixteen-gun *Albany*, a ship he considered totally unsuitable for an officer of his experience and demonstrated abilities. He called it "the worst calculated of any vessel in the King's service." Mowat decided to make the best of the situation, and as things turned out, he did remarkably well. He played a major role in the battle that resulted in one of the great defeats in American naval history.

Mowat was fortunate that the commander of the British land forces was another Scot, sixty-two-year-old General Francis McLean, described as a "cool, deliberate man." McLean also was an extremely capable officer who had distinguished himself as a courageous soldier fighting on the Continent against France and Spain. Over the course of a thirty-year career, he had participated in nineteen major battles. Three years into the American Revolution, his regiment was sent to Nova Scotia, and McLean was installed as military governor at Halifax, where his duties included overseeing Indian affairs and looking after arriving Loyalists.

Before the expedition set sail, Mowat was able to persuade Halifax port commander Vice Admiral James Gambier to temporarily add the thirty-two-gun frigate *Blonde* to his fleet for additional security. The fleet departed in early June 1779, with Mowat leading the way in his "wretched" flagship, HMS *Albany*.

En route, a continental naval force chased the British until they spotted *Blonde*, at which point they withdrew. Once again, Mowat's foresight had saved the day. However, the secrecy of the mission was compromised when news of the impending invasion force was relayed to Boston.

Two weeks later, on June 17, approximately 750 men in four transports, convoyed by three British sloops of war and *Blonde*, entered Penobscot Bay near Matinicus Island. After sailing up the bay, Mowat's fleet rounded the point at Dice Head (Jacob Dyce was an early Dutch settler) and entered the inner harbor of Bagaduce, a village of a few hundred souls surrounded by several sawmills.

Captain Mowat ordered two boats lowered, and a squad of Royal Marines accompanied by half a dozen Royal Engineers rowed ashore. The boats grated on a gravel beach, and the marines jumped out with their muskets primed. The British were ready for resistance, but to their surprise, the landing was unopposed.

In "A Journal of the Siege of Penobscot," Henry Mowat described the peninsula of Bagaduce: "A high ridge of land at that time much encumbered with wood. To its summit, where the fort was ordered to be erected there is an ascent of more than a quarter of a mile from the nearest shore of the harbor."

On board *Albany*, Mowat and McLean discussed their options when they realized there were no rebels defending the Bagaduce Peninsula. The situation was now reversed. The British were no longer the aggressors. Instead, they would have to defend the point against rebels, who they expected would attack them. Would they be able to set up a defensive position

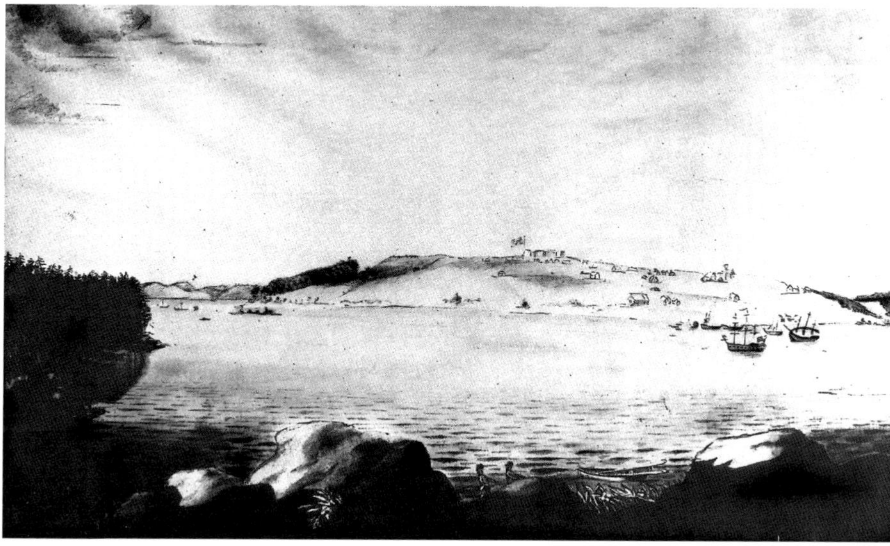

The Bagaduce Peninsula and Castine Harbor from Nautilus Island. Fort George is on the top of the hill flying the British flag. This sketch was made in 1780, a year after the abortive Penobscot Expedition. *Courtesy of the Castine Historical Society.*

in time? Mowat asked McLean to cancel or at least delay the departure of the frigate *Blonde*, which would give them additional protection. McLean acknowledged the legitimacy of Mowat's question but replied he lacked the authority to give the order.

As he watched *Blonde* sail away, Mowat realized the chances of his three small sloops successfully opposing an American naval force were slim. However, the resourceful captain had to work with what he had. He ordered a picket boat to stand off Cape Rosier to the south and relay word when a rebel fleet was sighted. In the meantime, he moored his ships in a line from Bagaduce to Banks Island (which was renamed Nautilus Island after one of Mowat's sloops) on the other side of the harbor.

The next few weeks became a whirlwind of activity for the British expedition. A contemporary journal tells us that Mowat and McLean received word on June 18 that "a fleet and army were preparing at Boston to besiege Penobscot." The two commanders realized they had only a limited amount of time to prepare their defenses before American forces appeared.

Realizing that General McLean needed all the help he could get, Captain Mowat sent sailors from his ships to work on the fort. A steady stream of boats ferried troops, tents, weapons and ammunition to shore. From

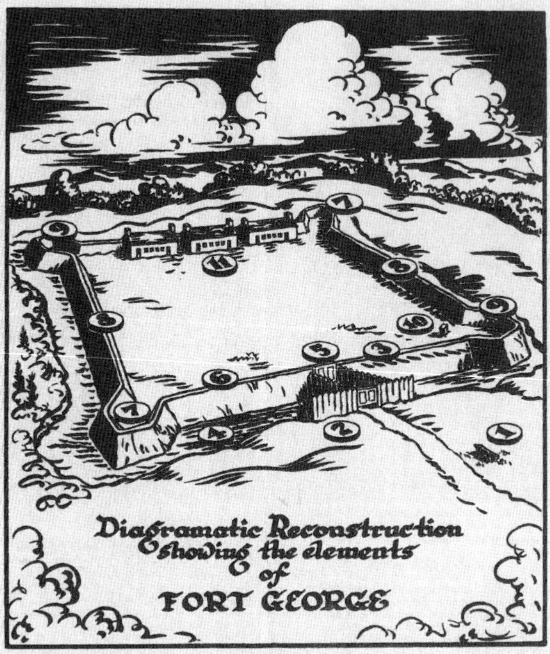

DIRECTORY OF FORT GEORGE MEMORIAL

1. Cannon
2. Palisade: A row of long pointed stakes for defense.
3. Fraising: Large stakes driven into rampart near the top, close together and sharply pointed. Extended horizontally half way across moat.
4. Moat: A ditch, here dug down to ledge.
5. Original Gateway facing the town.
6. Ramparts: These were six feet wide on top, and level.
7. Magazine: Built in this bastion. This one rebuilt in 1962. Over the original were layers of logs and all covered with earth.
8. Curtain: The ramparts connecting the flanks of the bastion.
9. Bastion: One on each corner, has two faces and two flanks.
10. Monument to British occupations.
11. Barracks: The British built a row of barracks parallel to northwest curtain.

Castine is an historic town and there are many points of interest worth visiting to the limit of time available to you. Some of these include:

1. The Wilson Museum—history, archeology, geology. Open daily 2-5 p.m. Summer.
2. Fort Madison, captured by British in War of 1812.
3. State of Maine Maritime Academy. Youth trained for merchant marine. Open daily 10-12 and 2-5.
4. Old Meeting House (1790) one of oldest in Maine. Unitarian. Revere Bell.
5. Old Courthouse—present library site.
6. Several old houses as far back as 1765. Not open to the public.

The Maine Department of Parks & Recreation hopes that your visit to Fort Kent Memorial has been pleasant. This folder is intended to make your visit more interesting and serve as a memento of your visit.

A sketch of Fort George built by the British defending the Bagaduce Peninsula. *Courtesy of the Castine Historical Society.*

there, materials were transported up the hill to the bluff. Earth works were laboriously dug as the troops battled swarms of mosquitos and black flies.

At the fort's location, some willing—and some unwilling—local residents were pressed into service to help the soldiers clear the land and construct primitive ramparts made mostly of earth and sod. Teams of oxen were drafted to pull out stumps and pull ship's cannon up the slope to where the outlines of a quadrangular-shaped fortress surrounded by ditches was under construction. It was named Fort George in honor of the king.

Meanwhile, Mowat surveyed the shoreline from the water, deciding where best to place cannon to oppose possible rebel landings. To the east, Bagaduce was protected by a long saltwater marsh that precluded the enemy from getting cannon into position to attack the fort. The western end of the peninsula had a steep bluff, which was climbable, but nevertheless presented a formidable obstacle.

The entrance to the harbor was flanked by Dice Point to the north and Nautilus (Banks) Island to the south. Mowat realized if he could prevent an

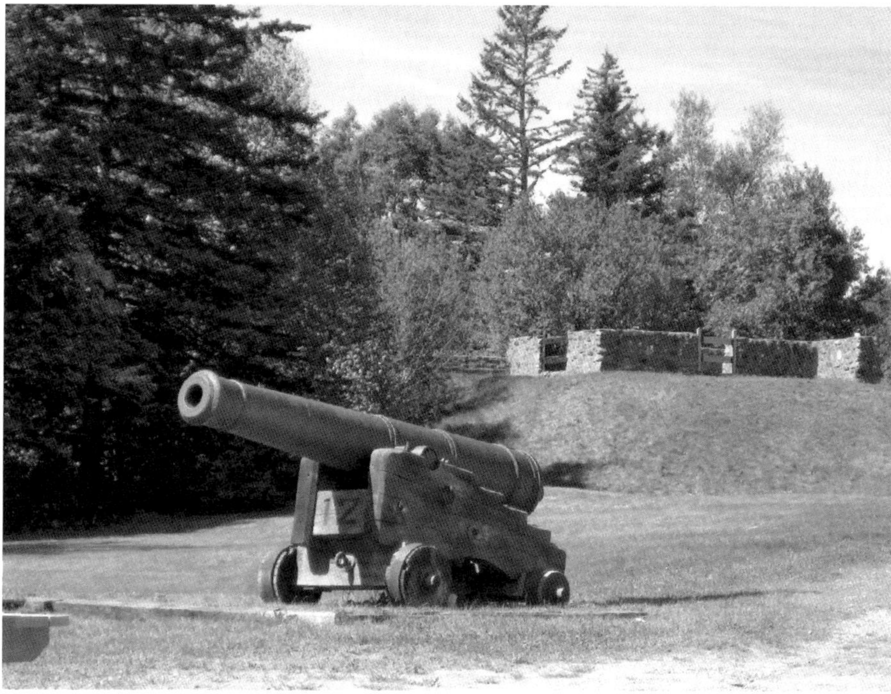

Cannon and earthworks at present-day Fort George. *Author's collection.*

invasion force from entering the harbor, he might be able to withstand the American assault until a British relief force arrived.

Bit by bit, Mowat formulated his defense plans in discussions with General McLean. They agreed the most vulnerable spot was a hard shingle beach on the southern shore. Both men realized this was the key to the defense of the British position and must be protected at all costs. Mowat ordered marines to take two cannon from his ships and mount them on a rise above the beach and place two more across the harbor on Nautilus Island.

The Massachusetts Response

Shortly after the British landed in Bagaduce, the news arrived in Boston. For the first time in more than three years, part of Massachusetts (in this case part of the Province of Maine) was in enemy hands, and alarm spread throughout the colony. On June 26, the Massachusetts General Court ordered the colony's board of war to organize an expeditionary force to dislodge the enemy. Interestingly, the Continental army under the control of George Washington was not asked for a single man, although the general approved of the mission. As Charles Bracelen Flood wrote, "This was to be virtually an all-Massachusetts show."

Orders were given to organize a force sufficient to oust the British garrison; it needed to be done quickly before the enemy had time to complete their fort. General Solomon Lovell of Weymouth, Massachusetts, was ordered to take command of the militia and march to the Penobscot along with one hundred artillerymen.

It soon became obvious that Lovell, a farmer turned legislator turned general, had little military experience. Second in command, however, was the capable Peleg Wadsworth, a former schoolteacher and the grandfather of Henry Wadsworth Longfellow. Wadsworth was described as a man "who was not apt to get rattled."

Colonel Paul Revere was placed in charge of the artillery. The energetic forty-four-year-old Revere was the finest silversmith in America and he knew it. The son of a French emigrant, he had participated in the Boston Tea Party in 1773, and his well-known midnight ride in 1775 spread the word of the British march to Lexington and Concord.

When the Revolution began, Revere joined the army and was stationed at Castle William in Boston Harbor, where he was placed in charge of an artillery unit. Revere soon tired of the relatively isolated life, and his intense personality created some friction with other officers. To relieve the boredom, he applied his engineering skills to maintaining the fort's armaments.

The entire Massachusetts navy of thirteen vessels, augmented by eight privateers and a warship from New Hampshire, was put under the command of Dudley Saltonstall, a cranky, obtuse commodore from Connecticut. It should be noted that several Massachusetts sea captains had turned down the offer before Saltonstall accepted. There were those who said Saltonstall was appointed because he was the captain of the largest ship in the fleet, the thirty-two-gun *Warren*.

John Paul Jones, who had previously served under Commodore Saltonstall, described him as "a sleepy gentleman who was also ill-natured and narrow-minded." Nevertheless, Saltonstall commanded an impressive armada, which mounted a total of 344 guns, to oppose Mowat's tiny squadron of three sloops, which carried 40 guns.

In a highly questionable decision, the Massachusetts War Board made Commodore Saltonstall commander of the expedition. Their unrealistic instructions to him stated: "You are to consult with the commander of the land forces [Lovell] that the Navy and Army may cooperate and assist each other…You will at all times study to promote the greatest harmony, peace and concord between the land and sea forces."

As stated, it was important that the expedition set sail before the British had time to strengthen Fort George and receive reinforcements from Halifax. Not surprisingly, organization proceeded fitfully. Men and equipment clogged the streets of Boston, and ships jammed the harbor as the largest amphibious operation of the war got underway.

William Fowler wrote an article in the 1979 *Harvard* magazine entitled "Disaster in Penobscot Bay" in which he described the situation. "The whole business turned out to be a classic example of how not to conduct a joint attack." Such operations require close cooperation and careful planning, and the American expedition lacked both. Fowler added, "Saltonstall did not have the vaguest notion about supporting a land operation, except to keep it at arm's length…Lines of authority were fuzzy, resulting in picayune squabbles over issues that made planning unpleasant and unproductive."

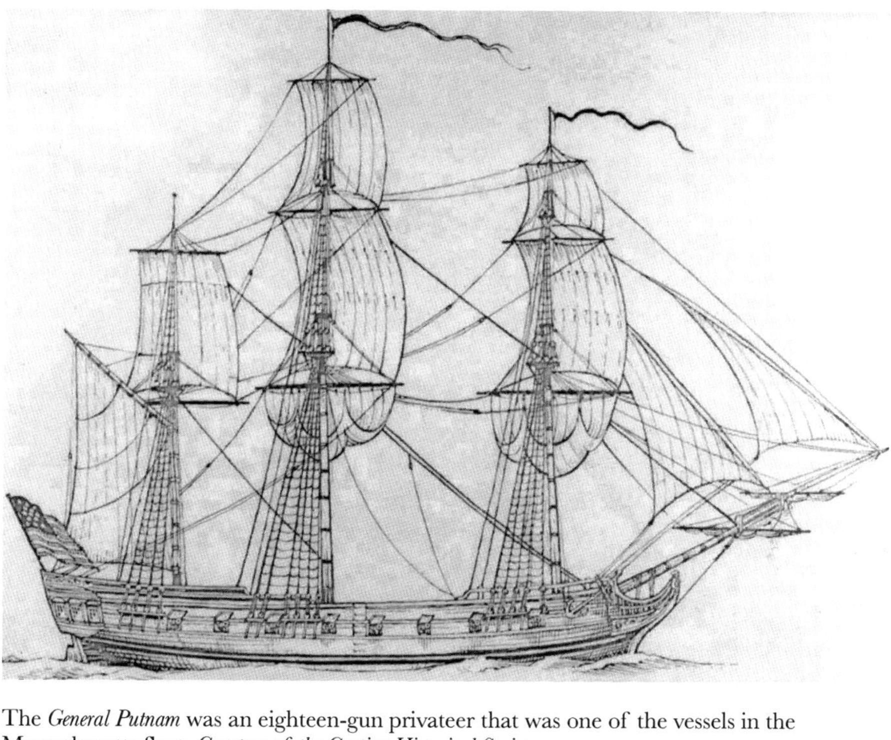

The *General Putnam* was an eighteen-gun privateer that was one of the vessels in the Massachusetts fleet. *Courtesy of the Castine Historical Society.*

The fleet of twenty-one war ships and twenty-five transport and cargo vessels was ordered to sail on July 12. Things did not go according to plan, and Saltonstall and Paul Revere did not leave Boston until July 19. Revere alone delayed departure by bringing a substantial amount of personal baggage. Ships left in stages and stopped at Boothbay Harbor, which was used as a gathering place until the entire expedition was assembled. Saltonstall and Revere finally arrived on July 21 in the flagship *Warren*, which was convoying the remaining transports.

When General Lovell went ashore at Boothbay to review his troops, he was shocked to discover that instead of the 1,500 men he had requested, he had 900, a quarter of whom Peleg Wadsworth described as "small boys and old men unfit for the service." By adding the sailors to these numbers, however, the optimistic Lovell felt they still had a force sufficient to defeat the British. Interestingly, one regiment was commanded by Samuel Thompson, Mowat's nemesis from his Falmouth days, who boasted "he would make the county too hot to hold" for those who did not volunteer to go along.

The following day, the expedition set sail for Penobscot Bay. Charles Bracelen Flood described the event: "Off they went, led by a farmer-legislator and a schoolteacher, their cannon commanded by a silversmith, their ships controlled by an unknown sea captain."

COMMODORE SALTONSTALL'S FOLLY

When General McLean received intelligence that "a fleet of near forty sail of vessels had sailed eastward from Boston," he sent an urgent message to Halifax asking for help. With a half-built fort, three sloops of war and four leaky transports, the British were clearly overmatched.

Thirty-eight days after the British arrived at Bagaduce, the Massachusetts/American fleet appeared in Penobscot Bay on July 25. Work on Fort George was still far from complete when Saltonstall sailed his fleet to the tip of the Bagaduce Peninsula. In his account of the upcoming siege, Mowat described the British fort. "The parapet was scarcely four feet high…The powder was lodged in holes dug in the proposed Glacis [an artificial slope of earth] and there was but a single gun mounted and that a six pounder."

When they got a closer look at the modest-sized fort, the American forces brimmed with confidence. General Lovell felt a quick victory was at hand and planned an assault the next day. One soldier was heard to say that he "could jump over them walls with a musket in each hand."

Commodore Saltonstall was not so confident. When he reconnoitered the British position from his flagship *Warren*, he saw that the British had contrived an ingenious defense of the harbor entrance, which was six hundred yards wide.

What Captain Mowat had done was to moor his sloops and rig lines between them so that they ranged bow to stern, across the entrance to the harbor. In this way, when Saltonstall attacked, the Americans would always face a British broadside. Behind his ships, Mowat anchored the four transports, armed with cannons from the sloops, as a second line of defense. Saltonstall took one look at the arrangement and, after firing a few shots, withdrew to consider his options.

Mowat modestly described his tactics in his journal:

> *The enemy came up and paraded before the entrance of the harbor in perfect confidence of entering it without difficulty; but there was such an excellent disposition made of the sloops of war and transports in the harbor as baffled every attempt of the enemy to force it for three days.*

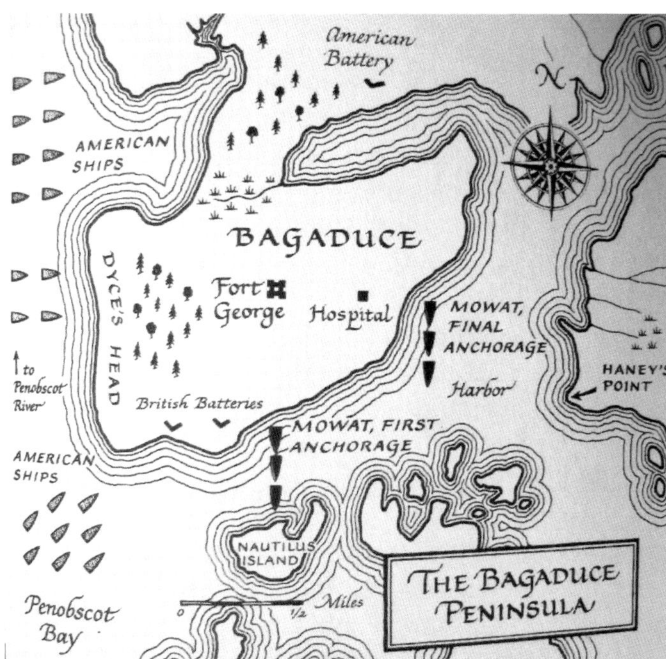

Henry Mowat's Fabian strategy in defending Castine's harbor kept Commodore Saltonstall's fleet from surrounding Fort George. *Courtesy of Charles Bracelen Flood, from his book* Rise and Fight Again.

Mowat continued:

> *These three or four days of Embarrassment on the part of the rebels gave our troops time to do something more to the Fort, to carry up the most necessary Stores, to mount several guns, and in short to devote every Endeavor to the present Exigency. The Enemy, having failed in their attempts on the harbor, effected at last a landing on the bluff, and by superior numbers forced our Pickets into the Fort.*

Mowat could see that Saltonstall and Lovell were unable to agree on a plan of battle. Should the American fleet first drive his sloops from their position at the entrance to the harbor or should the army launch an assault on the fort?

From the start, the American forces had a numerical advantage, but to the surprise of the British, they did not use it. Saltonstall sailed his ships back and forth in front of Mowat's sloops, exchanging fire but never drawing close enough to cause any real damage. In retrospect, there appeared to be little excuse for Saltonstall's timidity. (He would later be court martialed for his caution.)

In Saltonstall's defense, the privateer captains in his fleet were reluctant to risk their ships when they realized that Fort George contained no loot. When they saw there was little to be gained and everything to be lost, their ships in particular, their enthusiasm for the enterprise waned. One privateer captain stated that "he had rather all the Penobscot Expedition would go to hell than he would lose the benefits of his cruiser." He and other captains had plans for other coastal forays, which they hoped would yield more lucrative opportunities.

However, the captains of the regular ships in the Massachusetts/American navy were disgusted with the inactivity and signed a petition urging Commodore Saltonstall to "go immediately into the Harbor and attack the Enemy ships. We think Delays in the present Case are extremely dangerous as our enemies are daily fortifying and strengthening themselves."

The delays also exasperated the American militia, and some began to desert. Colonel John Brewer was a local resident who knew the weaknesses of the British position and was sympathetic to the American cause; Brewer urged Saltonstall to conduct an immediate land and sea assault, which could be successful "in half an hour."

The reply was typical Saltonstall. "You seem to be damned knowing in this matter. I am not going to risk my shipping in that damned hole"—and he did not. When the commander of another ship agreed with Brewer, Saltonstall threatened to degrade his vessel to a "bread ship."

As long as Mowat's flotilla remained anchored in the harbor, the inexperienced and insecure General Lovell considered his numbers too few to mount the steep incline at the end of the peninsula and seize the fort. The argument raged back and forth, with Saltonstall unwilling to risk his ships in support of Lovell's troops.

Peleg Wadsworth decided to act, apparently independently, and on July 27, he landed a small force of marines on Nautilus Island. The British were driven from their battery, and their cannons were captured. The next day, Wadsworth's marines began to bombard Mowat's sloops in the harbor from this location. This forced Mowat to move his line of sloops farther back into the harbor and out of range.

A British sergeant named Lawrence described the situation in his journal:

> *This morning they opened a battery at Nautilus Island and began to show their rebellious spirit by firing on our ships, fort and Batteries. We did not spare Powder and Ball in responding. There was two men wounded on board the ships. One of their shot sent into our fort, which killed a bullock on the parade ground. Thus they finished the day's malice.*

During the withdrawal, Mowat realized that his ship's cannon on the opposite side of the deck from the harbor entrance were useless. In a practical move, he ordered them taken ashore and used to strengthen the defenses of Fort George.

After two days of quarreling with Saltonstall, General Lovell finally persuaded the cautious commodore to provide support for a night attack on July 28. The reluctant Saltonstall was still not happy with the idea, but a majority of his officers approved of the plan and he grudgingly agreed to go along with Lovell's strategy.

At 4:00 a.m., a bombardment from the American ships shattered the morning stillness. The barrage preceded the landing of 250 marines and 400 militia on the beach at Dice Head at the western end of the Bagaduce Peninsula. Charles Bracelen Flood described the scene:

> *Every kind of thing was being thrown at the defenders, solid metal balls weighing twelve and eighteen pounds, grape shot, smaller deadly balls, bar shot, wicked iron dumbbells that skipped from spot to spot on landing,*

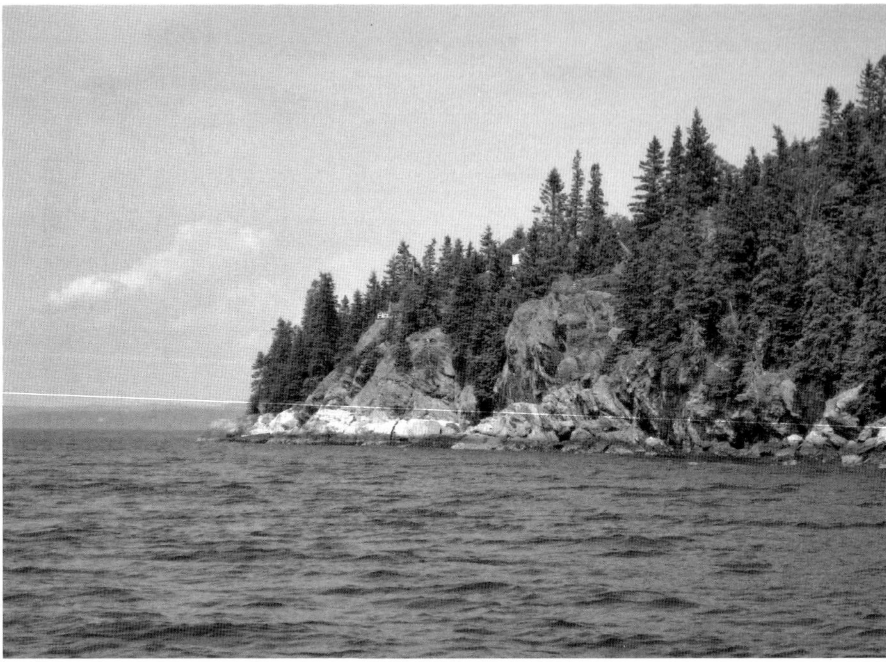

In the face of heavy fire, the attacking American force scaled the bluff at Dice Head on the western end of the Bagaduce Peninsula. *Author's collection.*

> *chopping any flesh they encountered. For half an hour the gun crews of the fleet sweated and grunted.*

Up on the bluff, 150 members of the Argyll Highlanders regiment crouched behind the rocks and trees, ready to oppose the Americans' landing force. The Scottish officer in charge sent a messenger back to General McLean at Fort George requesting reinforcements, but the courier got lost in the thick underbrush.

Peleg Wadsworth described the American landing:

> *The fire of the enemy opened upon us from the top of the bank. As we stepped out there was a shower of musketry in our faces from the top of the cliff. We soon found the cliff insurmountable even without opponents. The party therefore was divided into three parts. One sent to the left, another to the right and the center keeping up their fire to amuse the enemy.*

In twenty minutes of bitter fighting, however, the numerically superior Americans forced their way up the bank and drove the British from their positions. The cost was heavy. More than one hundred Americans were killed or wounded, while British casualties numbered about thirty.

When his troops reached the top of Dice Head, General Lovell sent a message to Saltonstall:

> *This morning I have made my landing on the head of the peninsula, which is three hundred feet high.* [Paul Revere thought it was closer to two hundred feet high.] *After a very smart conflict we put them to the rout and they left the woods with a number of killed and wounded. We hope soon to have the satisfaction of capturing the whole army.*

This was not to be. The closer his forces got to Fort George, the more formidable it looked. General Lovell sent a message to Saltonstall on the *Warren* requesting reinforcements. Receiving no response to the note, Lovell told his men to dig in and prepare for a siege.

Had the American troops realized how close they were to victory, they would have continued with their attack. When General McLean saw scores of enemy soldiers appearing in the woods near the unfinished walls of Fort George, he moved to the flagpole and prepared to raise a white flag in surrender. Then, to his surprise, the American attack slowed and stopped. Years later, McLean wrote, "I was not going to needlessly sacrifice the lives of my young soldiers. It would be better for them to sit out the war as prisoners of war."

In retrospect, Lovell's problem was that having no direction or support from Saltonstall, he had no plan beyond getting his men ashore and digging in. Charles Bracelen Flood speculates what might have happened had Lovell continued with his attack:

> *If the troops had attacked, Fort George would have surrendered. Seven hundred British soldiers, three warships and four transports and their crews would have been captured. Every American objective of the Penobscot Expedition would have been achieved. It would have been a stunning victory bought for less than twenty lives…It would probably have marked the end of England's effort to control this sector of the American coast.*

Later that morning, Commodore Saltonstall finally made a token attack when several of his ships began to fire at Mowat's sloops, albeit at long range. Mowat's ships replied, and an artillery duel developed between the two fleets separated by about a mile. This was at the same time the American attack on land began to slow down.

Mowat's ships anchored in the harbor gave better than they received. William Fowler wrote in the *Harvard* magazine article, "The British gunners—with a better eye, more experience, and a good deal of luck—put two shots into *Warren*'s mainmast and another into her bowsprit." Some of *Warren*'s lines were "cut to pieces," and the forestay was "shot away." The damage to *Warren* was not critical, but it was serious enough to cause the frigate to nearly run the on the rocks. The cautious Saltonstall sailed his vessel out of danger and withdrew for two days to make repairs.

In the meantime, General McLean brought more cannon from the now unused transport ships in the harbor to strengthen Fort George. Despite the efforts of the American artillery to destroy the fort, its walls, made mostly of earth and sod, acted as a cushion. Cannonballs fired from the American ships did not send splinters of wood and stone flying in every direction but simply sank into the soil.

What were Paul Revere's actions during the campaign? We know that he was involved in the successful attack on Nautilus (Banks) Island led by Peleg Wadsworth on July 26, and the next day he oversaw the transport of guns during the assault on Dice Point. Curiously, in the middle of the American attack, Revere left his men on the beach and had himself rowed out to his ordinance brig *Samuel* for a midday dinner with the ship's officers.

Revere returned to shore in midafternoon and was credited with making a valuable suggestion for hauling cannon to the top of the one-hundred-foot-high bluff and positioning them to bombard the fort. In the opinion of many, at that point, he should have remained on shore for the duration of the assault. However, the peripatetic silversmith returned to the brig *Samuel*, where he had supper and spent the night. Meanwhile, the rest of his artillerymen remained ashore and under fire.

The next day, Colonel Revere was asked to supply ramrods, ammunition and sponges so that the cannon captured from the British could be turned against their former owners. Revere turned down the appeal, saying that the supplies were needed aboard *Samuel*, which was questionable. The request was passed along to the gunnery officer on the *Warren*, who for some reason covered for Revere, and the necessary materials were sent ashore.

Not surprisingly, Revere's cavalier behavior was causing resentment among his fellow officers as well as among the men. When word reached General Lovell, he issued an order for Lieutenant Colonel Paul Revere "to come on shore and en camp with his men."

Revere was not happy with the command, but on July 30, he went ashore with the tents and baggage he had brought from Boston. In spite of Lovell's orders, Revere continued to have himself rowed out to *Samuel* every day, where he would change into a clean shirt and have dinner with the ship's officers.

After a siege of three weeks, soldiers on both sides were becoming exhausted. Their diaries described what had become a stalemate:

> *A brisk cannonade the whole day…Slack fire between the fortress and the batteries on the heights…Only a few cannon shot exchanged, by reason of heavy rain…Cannonading the greatest part of the day…This morning commenced with the common game of exchanging shot on both sides… Some skirmishing at daybreak…A smart cannonading from all the batteries well directed…The men are very much fatigued.*

It was generally agreed that Commodore Saltonstall had more than enough ships to successfully attack and sink Mowat's three little sloops. His reluctance to do so had serious consequences for the success of the campaign. While Mowat controlled the harbor, the British continued to strengthen Fort George.

Both sides were sustaining frequent casualties, although the ensuing siege particularly wore down Lovell's militiamen, who were running short of supplies and ammunition. The besieged British garrison held out, sustained by the expectation of a relief force. It is probably unfair to place the entire blame for the expedition's failure on Commodore Saltonstall, but clearly his excessive caution was a major factor.

SIR GEORGE COLLIER TO THE RESCUE

In early August, Saltonstall received a message that a British relief expedition from New York was on the way. The frustrated General Lovell continued to press the commodore to take action before it was too late and sent him the following message: "The information that British ships have sailed is not to be despised. Not a moment is to be lost…I shall impatiently await your reply."

Following another council of war, General Lovell wrote in his journal, "I wish it in my power to act more offensively." Shortly after this, Saltonstall received the following communiqué from the Massachusetts War Board:

> *We have for some time been at a loss to know why the enemy's ships have not been attacked...It is agreed on all hands that they are in your power. Why should any business be delayed to another day? Our apprehensions of your danger have ever been from a reinforcement to the enemy...It is therefore our orders that you take the most effectual measures for the capture or destruction of the enemy's ships, with the greatest dispatch.*

The beleaguered Saltonstall finally gave in, and after three weeks of indecision and more than a dozen fruitless councils of war, he agreed to a full-scale assault. Ominously, the date was Friday, August 13.

The American strategy was for Lovell's forces to drive a wedge between Fort George and Mowat's ships, which by now had withdrawn to the back of the harbor. At the same time, Saltonstall would take five of his ships and, led by the *Warren*, attack Mowat's little fleet and cut them off from the land forces.

In the harbor, Mowat received information from a deserter that something was afoot. A Loyalist doctor, John Calef, surgeon to the British garrison, recorded in his journal what transpired: "He [Mowat] brought a transport into the line [with the sloops] and fitted it out with what guns that could be procured. Captain Mowat next added marines to his ships, double-shotted his guns and made every disposition for the most vigorous defense." Lastly, he ordered the remaining three transports scuttled to keep them from falling into enemy hands.

Lovell began his attack at 2:00 p.m. on August 14. His troops were successfully advancing on the fort when Saltonstall received a message that sails were seen coming up the bay from the south. The American commander was expecting reinforcements, but there was also the possibility that the ships might be British. As a precaution, Saltonstall immediately called off the attack and hastily called another council-of-war. Mowat wrote in his log, "The appearance of some strange sails in the offing, disconcerted the Enemy's plan and the five ships stood off."

By ten o'clock that night, Saltonstall knew that the "strange sails" were British yet surprisingly he did not communicate the information to Lovell. It turned out that the squadron was under the command of Commodore Sir George Collier, ten days out of New York. It consisted of the sixty-four-gun *Raisonable*, which was superior to any of the American warships; three frigates; and three sloops. When Lovell finally found this out at midnight he immediately gave orders for his men to evacuate the peninsula.

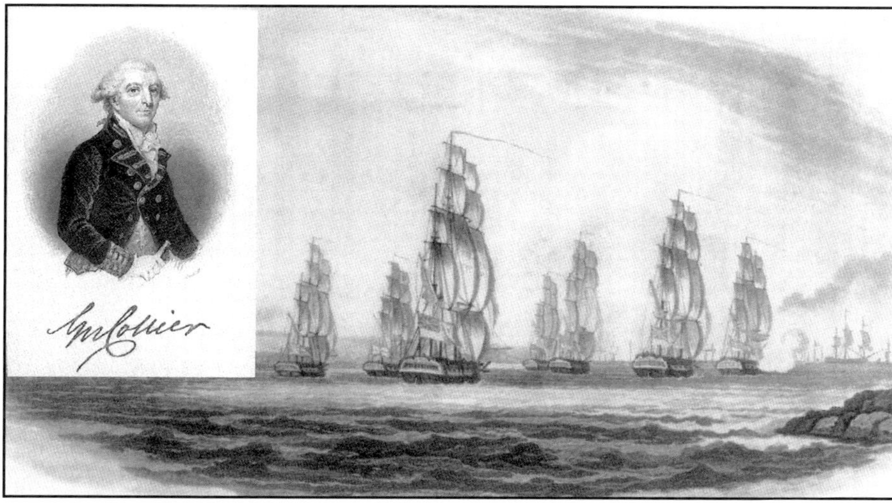

British Commodore Sir George Collier's fleet arrived just in time to keep Fort George from falling to the American attack. The American fleet is seen retreating in the distance. *Courtesy of the National Maritime Museum, Greenwich, England.*

Charles Bracelen Flood observed, "Lovell pulled off a military miracle. Starting at midnight in a rainstorm 750 marines were moved to the beach and ferried out to the ships before dawn with all their equipment." To his credit, Paul Revere was able to remove most of the artillery pieces safely onto the ships. The following morning, British scouting parties issuing from Fort George were amazed to find the entire American army had slipped away.

The next day, August 15, Saltonstall drew his ships up in a crescent formation between Bagaduce and Islesboro, while Wadsworth supervised the loading of transports preparatory to what he anticipated would be an orderly withdrawal up the Penobscot River. Saltonstall had originally planned to challenge the advancing British squadron. Watching the British advance led by the ship-of-the-line *Raisonable*, he apparently lost his nerve. Perhaps he realized that his crews could never stand up to Commodore Collier's well-trained gunners. William Fowler, in the *Harvard Magazine*, suggests he also must have realized he could never have gotten the dozen privateersmen to join him in a straightforward battle.

Collier aboard *Raisonable* expected "the rebel fleet to dispute our passage." Instead he was amazed to see the American fleet disintegrate before his eyes. An assortment of forty odd American ships fled up the Penobscot River. The faster warships and privateers soon overtook the twenty-four lumbering transports. During the next few hours, one after another of the American ships ran ashore or were captured by the British. Saltonstall's flagship *Warren* sailed fifteen miles up the river to Winterport, where it grounded and was set on fire.

As Collier's ships swept past Bagaduce, Mowat's little fleet of three sloops burst from the harbor that they had been successfully defending for so long. After weeks of being boxed in, they were eager to finally take the offensive. During the next few hours Mowat joined in the pursuit, destroying and capturing several American ships.

When the British fleet drew near, General Lovell came alongside *Warren* in his barge to ask Saltonstall for reassurances that the American warships would cover the troop transports as they retreated up the Penobscot River. The commodore's response was to sail his flagship past the astonished Lovell and head up the river, passing the troop and supply ships in the process.

The battle was over before it had begun. That night, General Lovell bitterly described the scene in his diary:

> *The transports weighted anchor and to our great mortification they were soon followed by our Men of Wars, pursued by only four of the enemy's ships…To attempt to give a description of this terrible day is out of my power…To see four ships pursuing seventeen sail of armed vessels, nine of which are stout ships, transports on fire, Men of War blowing up, provisions of all kinds and every kind of store on the shore and as much confusion as can possibly be conceived.*

As the American ships grounded along the banks of the Penobscot, soldiers and sailors scrambled ashore and fled into the woods in an effort to escape. The next day, the river was filled with scuttled American ships and the banks were littered with the remains of vessels that had been run ashore and burned. A total of seventeen American vessels were burned or blown up while another twenty-eight were captured.

Of the entire American fleet, the only ship that put up a fight was *Hampden*, the state ship of New Hampshire. It squared off with the thirty-two-gun frigate *Blonde*. Unfortunately, the sloop of twenty-two guns proved to be no match for the British vessel. After an hour of bloody fighting, Captain Titus Salter hauled down the flag, and his crew of 130 men was taken prisoner.

General Wadsworth repeatedly attempted to rally the militia when they came ashore, but his orders were ignored as panicked men and officers fled past him into the woods. At one point, he told Paul Revere to mount cannon

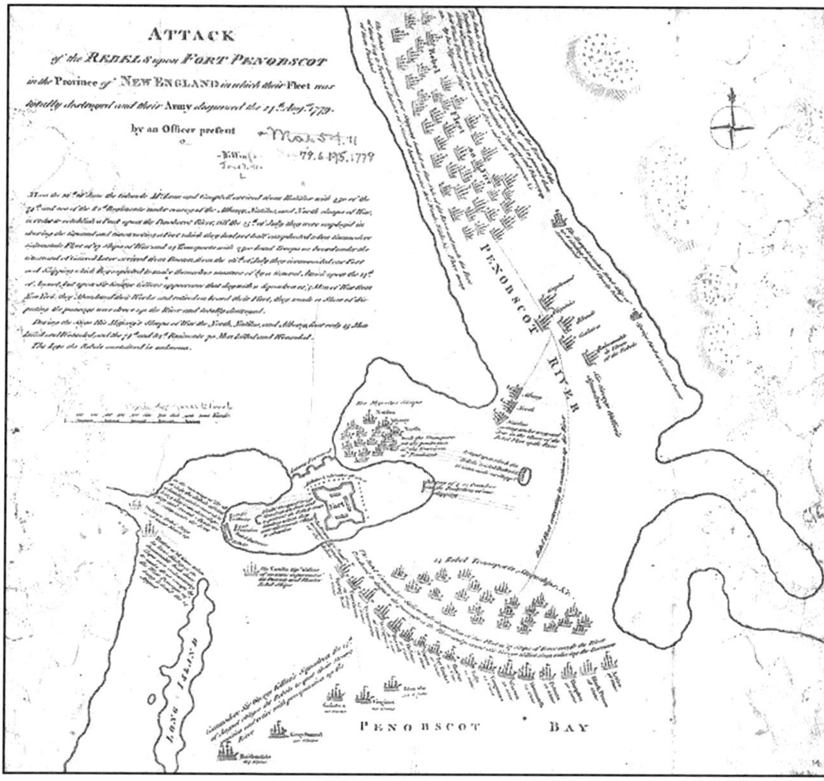

A chart showing the relative positions of the two fleets and the American retreat up the Penobscot River. *Courtesy of the Castine Historical Society.*

on the riverbank to oppose the British advance, but Revere ignored his order. Instead, he loaded a barge with his baggage from the ordinance brig *Samuel* and had it rowed upstream.

Wadsworth described their exchange:

> *I was directly opposed by Lieutenant Colonel Revere who said that I had no right to command either him or the boat and gave orders to the contrary…The reason he gave was that he had all his private baggage at stake. I asked him whether he came there to take care of his private baggage or serve the State.*

Paul Revere continued to make no effort to help Wadsworth. Instead, he headed upstream with two officers and eight crewmen in his barge, abandoning the rest of his men as well as the *Samuel*. The next day, Revere also ignored General Lovell's order to set up an artillery position at the falls of the Penobscot. Instead, he reportedly told a ship's captain he was "going home."

The self-centered and irresponsible Colonel Revere, indignant at also having lost his luggage, struggled forty miles through the woods to the site of present-day Augusta on the Kennebec River. After three days of walking, Revere's feet had become so sore he could go no further. He gave his men money for their return march and, with several officers, hired a boat to take them down the Kennebec to the sea and hence to Boston.

As the British ships, with Henry Mowat's sloops in the vanguard, advanced up the Penobscot River, they captured a number of the American vessels that were salvageable. Although many ships had been destroyed, others had simply been run aground and deserted by their crews.

In retrospect, one could argue that had Saltonstall and Revere supported Lovell and Wadsworth in their attempts to defend the American position along the banks of the Penobscot, the expedition's dismal failure, which resulting in the death or capture of an estimated five hundred Americans, could have been averted.

During the next month, hundreds of American soldiers and sailors straggled back through the wilderness to their homes in Massachusetts and southern Maine, some dying of exposure and starvation along the way. "Our retreat was as badly managed as the whole expedition has been," wrote a young marine. Henry Mowat observed in his diary, "The crews made the best of their way to New England, through the woods, in the utmost distress."

The Conclusion of the Campaign

The Penobscot defeat was the worst naval loss suffered by America in the Revolution and one of the most disastrous in the country's history. Although it did not affect the outcome of the war, it discouraged further military advances by the New England colonies to the north. Henry Mowat wrote, "Every thought of attempting to take Canada and Nova Scotia was thenceforth laid aside and the trade and transports from the banks of Newfoundland along the coast of Nova Scotia enjoyed unusual security."

Mowat and his flotilla had played a large part in establishing a place for American Loyalists to live, as well as saving the eastern provinces of

Nova Scotia, New Brunswick and Newfoundland from further incursions. It was acknowledged that his stubborn defense of Bagaduce harbor had given Colliers's relief squadron time to sail to the Penobscot. Under the circumstances, Captain Mowat might well have expected more in the way of recognition from Commodore George Collier.

Mowat's victory, however, gained him little professionally. Charles Bracelen Flood writes, "One of the victors was in a rage." After years of service, Henry Mowat thought he would finally receive proper recognition. It was a common naval practice that, after a victory, the senior officer would be sent to England with dispatches. As the naval officer who had done more than any other to achieve the victory, Mowat rightfully expected to return to London to report on the triumph. It was a significant honor to be selected, and often, the carrier of the news received a promotion and an audience with the king.

George Collier, however, had other plans. He told Mowat, "No, you are too important here." Mowat was informed, "It is with the utmost regret he [Collier] could not spare a ship from the station." Collier reassured Mowat that if he did send an officer to England, he would have chosen the erstwhile captain. In reality, after ordering Mowat's ship *Albany* up the Penobscot River to collect cannon and supplies from the American wrecks, Collier surreptitiously dispatched another ship to England bearing his own account of the victory. This done, Collier immediately departed for New York.

In Collier's report to the admiralty, he made no mention of the heroic contributions of Mowat's little flotilla nor did he include the names of the ship's captains. In New York, Henry Clinton was equally indifferent to Mowat's services when he heard the news of the victory. Partial to a fellow army officer, he elaborated on General McLean's role and said nothing in his narrative of the important role played by Mowat in the victory.

Finally, when Admiral Arbuthnot replaced Sir George Collier, Henry Mowat might have hoped he would at last receive recognition from the admiralty for his services on the Penobscot. Sadly, none were forthcoming. As Mowat wrote in his journal, he had "the distress of seeing every promotion made by this Admiral, without exception, was of officers junior to him."

In sum, Mowat's superiors agreed with one historian's view of the affair that "Mowat's contribution to the British victory at Penobscot was negligible." It would appear that he was still being made the scapegoat for following Admiral Graves's orders when he burned Falmouth in 1775. The British high command had a long memory.

As the survivors trekked slowly back through the woods, letters describing the disaster reached Boston ahead of them. Disbelief and dismay were followed by anger. The expedition had cost Massachusetts an estimated $7 million, including the loss of every warship belonging to the colony. Who was to blame? General John Sullivan, from New Hampshire, summed up public opinion when he said, "The expense of the expedition was not so distressing as the disgrace."

A board of inquiry was established to determine what had gone wrong. When Commodore Saltonstall returned to Boston, he refused to appear, stating that he was an officer in the Continental Navy and that Massachusetts did not have jurisdiction over him. As a result, the commodore was court-martialed by the Board of Continental Navy Captains who found him "rightly responsible for the total destruction of the fleet due to his not exerting himself at the time of the retreat or opposing the enemy's foremost ships in pursuit." Saltonstall was immediately discharged from the navy. At the same time, many newspapers demanded an even stiffer punishment.

General Wadsworth was called before the board. His actions were praised, and he was found to have "comported himself with great activity, courage and prudence." General Lovell was also absolved of responsibility for the defeat, and it was announced, "He had not been properly supported by Commodore Saltonstall."

When marine captain T.J. Carnes was called to testify, he was candid in his account of Paul Revere's behavior throughout the campaign. Carnes gave a detailed description of Colonel Revere's actions, beginning with his spending the night aboard *Samuel* and concluding with his disobedience of orders during the retreat. Upon his return to Boston, General Lovell further supported Carnes's accusations.

Revere was temporarily placed under house arrest, although he protested that he was the victim of rumor and false accusations. He brazenly insisted on a review of his case, which indecisively concluded his behavior was "not wholly justifiable." After the Revolution, Revere persisted in trying to clear his name and received a more favorable ruling from another court martial: "That Colonel Revere be acquitted with equal honor as were the other officers in the expedition." The reprieve fooled no one, since by now, everyone wanted to forget the Penobscot Expedition.

MOWAT ON THE PENOBSCOT: A PERSONAL VIEW

The previously mentioned Colonel John Brewer was a resident of the Bagaduce Peninsula who became friendly with Henry Mowat during the course of the Penobscot campaign. Mowat had made it clear to the residents of the area that they would be left alone as long as they stayed out of the conflict. When wounded from the sunken American ships were brought ashore to the settlement, Brewer requested safe passage for them to Boston in a chartered schooner.

In fact, one of the wounded was George Ross, a celebrated rebel ship captain, who Mowat was searching for. The following letter, written by Loyalist David Perham, details Colonel Brewer's account of the interactions he had with Henry Mowat regarding Ross. The way the letter is written can be confusing in that Perham sometimes refers to Colonel Brewer as "I" and sometimes as "Brewer." More importantly, however, it gives us an insight into the volatility of Captain Mowat's character and personality. Excerpts follow.

> *In a few days Captain Mowat came up the river and anchored his ship off my cove. At night when I came down, I was hailed, gave my name and told them I lived abreast of the ship commanded by Captain Mowat… He frequently called me on board when I was passing and enquired after the sick and the wounded and often invited me into his cabin to take a glass of wine or brandy. This friendship subsisted till the schooner was completed* [loaded].
>
> *Brewer had received permission from General Francis McLean to make up a list of the sick and wounded for approval so that they might be sent home to their friends to Boston and other places. I had heard of George Ross* [the rebel captain], *who had been wounded the day he landed. Brewer perpetuated a sharp trick by handing in a Captain by the name of Ross, whom he entered by name, without his military prefix. I presented the General* [McLean] *with my list, then returned home late at night, much fatigued with the hour.*
>
> *Before I got home Ichabod Colson informed Captain Mowat what I had done with Captain Ross. Mowat upon hearing this was enraged and probably somewhat loaded with "Dutch Courage" from the brandy he had in his cabin. He thus vented his feeling upon me at our meeting the next morning.*
>
> *The first compliment I received was, "You damned rebel. I understand you stopped at Marsh Bay and took on board Captain Ross, one of the*

finest officers there was in the navy. I meant to have kept him and would have given two of my captains for him."

"Did you return him as a Captain?" "No, I returned him as George Ross." Making use of the same opprobrious language he added, "Did you not know that I had not given you orders to take any man on board?" I answered "yes."

"Then" said he, with his sword flourishing over my head, "how dare you do it?" "Because," said I, "I received my orders another way!" "Which way," said he? I answered, "From General McLean, your master!"

It may well be supposed from my answer that I was somewhat agitated.

He stepped back and drawing his sword out of its scabbard, said, "You d——d rebel! I have a good mind to run you through." I opened my breast and told him, "There is your mark, do it if you dare! I am in your power."

He turned on his heel and stepped back a little, then turned and advanced flourishing his sword with more passion than could well be expressed and said, "Before sunrise tomorrow morning, your buildings shall be laid in ashes." I told him it was in his power to do it but I asked him what he thought I should be doing in the meantime. Upon which he turned on his heel again and marched off to his boat and I to mine.

I came home and told Mrs. Brewer what had passed, so that she might not be surprised if he proceeded to put his threat in execution, though I did not believe he would. However, we did not have so good a night's rest as usual.

The next day I saw Captain Mowat come ashore at my landing, which put Mrs. Brewer in a panic. He walked along very moderately to my door where Mrs. Brewer was introduced to him. He took a seat and made himself extremely entertaining by a social conversation for two or three hours and took coffee. He enquired into the situation of the family, how many children we had, our financial circumstances and offered to get provisions for them at the port area at Halifax.

Colonel Brewer stated that with the above exception, he [Mowat] *always appeared very friendly. Soon after his arrival he called all hands on deck* [of *Albany*] *and, in my presence, told them if they took one thing out of my garden or field they should be punished. His crew strictly adhered to his orders during their whole stay. I supplied him with milk, garden vegetables and pigeons for his cabin, which he generously paid for in money.*

Perham's letter indicates that, although Captain Mowat was an impulsive man, there were redeeming traits in his character. His conduct toward Brewer shows that he did not hold a grudge. In time, the two men resumed a cordial relationship.

AFTERMATH

Henry Mowat remained on station along the Maine coast until 1782. The winter of 1779–80 was brutally cold, and in January 1780, Penobscot Bay was frozen solid. Mowat's kindness in arranging food and shelter for the countless suffering families in the area was duly noted and appreciated. For them, the "Mad Mowat" label, associated with his burning of Falmouth, no longer applied. It was understood by many of the residents that back in 1775, he was simply an officer carrying out distasteful orders.

Although the British continued to hold Bagaduce for the remainder of the war, they remained on their guard. General McLean continued to reinforce Fort George, employing his soldiers as well as local residents. By the time frigid weather arrived in January 1780, the garrison was comfortably housed in their barracks.

The next spring, General Wadsworth was placed in command of "the Eastern parts," i.e., Maine. Determined to revenge the humiliations of the previous summer's campaign, he organized an expedition to sail up the Penobscot River to recover cannons from the American ships that had been scuttled.

Wadsworth successfully completed his mission and was heading down river when Henry Mowat spotted him as he was passing Fort George. The vigilant captain chased him across Penobscot Bay to Camden, where the pursuit was stopped by a detachment of American troops. A newspaper account reported, "Mowat was 'obliged to meach [sulk] back, impoverished by the loss of two sloops, eight cannon and forty men.'" Wadsworth's raid was proclaimed a significant achievement in the press.

The next winter, the British returned the favor and captured the unsuspecting General Wadsworth at his home near Camden. He was taken to Bagaduce and imprisoned at Fort George. Following a lengthy incarceration, he and a fellow prisoner escaped by cutting a hole in the ceiling of their jail, climbing over the walls of the fort and making their way to safety.

In October 1780, residents on the Penobscot Bay island of Islesboro were astonished to see a small boat approaching HMS *Albany* bearing a flag of truce. On board was a determined young science professor named Fortescue Vernon from Harvard College. The previous summer, Fortescue's mentor, Reverend Professor Williams, realized that an eclipse of the sun would occur in October and would be visible along the eastern coast of the Province of Maine. War or no war, the Harvard scientists were not to miss the event.

Reverend Professor Williams sent Fortescue Vernon and six students to record the event. They arrived in mid-October, carrying a letter from Reverend Williams stating, "Their business was solely to promote the interest of science, which is the common interest of all mankind."

Peleg Wadsworth (before he was captured) gave them permission to proceed into Penobscot Bay under a flag of truce. *Albany* captain Henry Mowat's response was also friendly and courteous. Colonel Campbell, described as "a violent, passionate fellow," was less welcoming: "Come up ye Bay immediately, anchor ye vessel in Williams Cove…Have no communication with ye inhabitants and depart on ye 28th day of ye month."

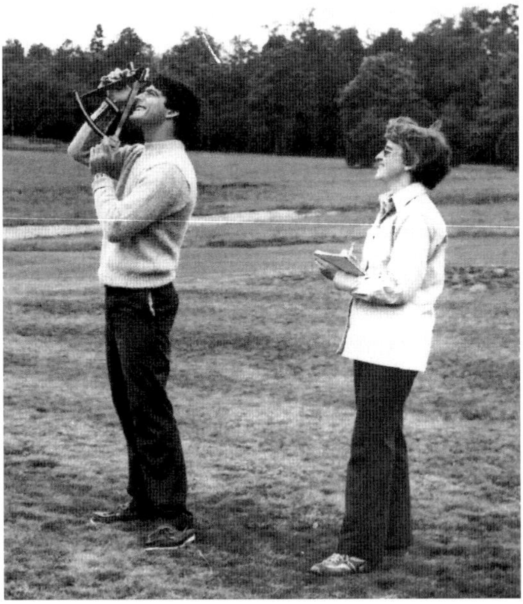

A reenactment of the eclipse was conducted in 1980 by Harvard scientists Gordon Schiff and Barbara Hughes, who used eighteenth-century technology to commemorate the 200th anniversary of the event. *Courtesy of the Islesboro Historical Society.*

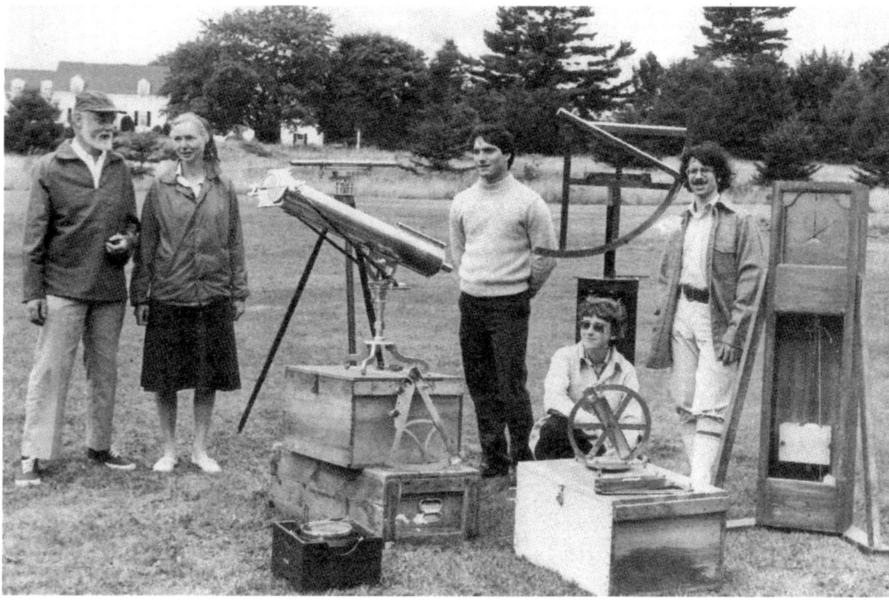

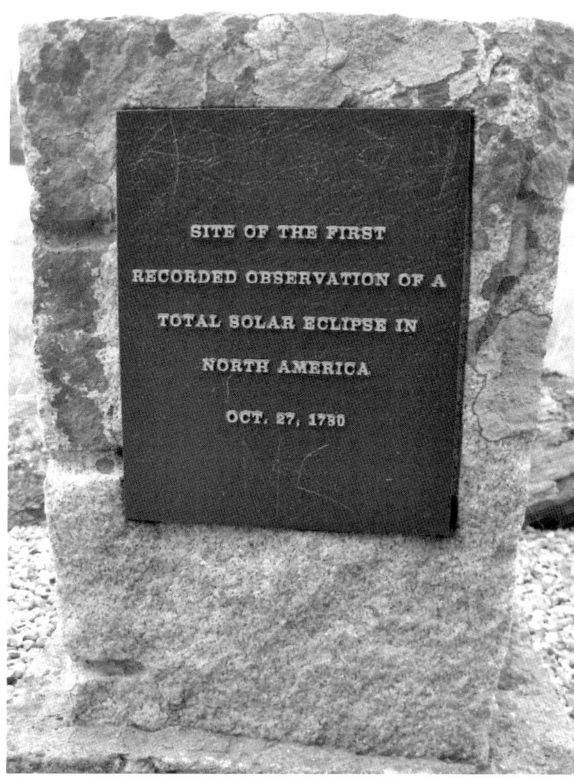

Top: These are examples of the instruments used to measure an eclipse of the sun in 1780 on Islesboro. *Courtesy of the Islesboro Historical Society*.

Right: A plaque on Islesboro marks the place where the observation took place. *Author's collection.*

Although the party was forbidden to communicate with local inhabitants, Islesboro resident Shubael Williams was not intimidated by Colonel Campbell's bluster and turned over his barn and part of his house to the scientists. The Harvard men set up their telescopes in the barn, and Mrs. Williams prepared their meals while Shubael kept an eye out for uninvited British visitors.

A thick fog blanketed the coast for a week, but on the morning of October 27, the weather cleared and a perfect day dawned for the viewing. Apparently the eclipse was "a wondrous experience" for the scientists, who wrote down detailed observations before departing the next day. Today on Islesboro, a granite shaft marks the spot where they stood.

After serving on the North Atlantic coast for almost twenty-eight years, Henry Mowat was permitted to return to England in 1782. Sitting in a chilly London flat, the disaffected officer began a letter of grievance to the king outlining his frustrations at not receiving a faster promotion. Mowat stated, "His feelings as a man, his spirit and honor as an officer and his duty to the service were injured and degraded...Circumstances compel me to consider resignation from the service."

But Mowat did not resign. After meeting with the Board of the Admiralty, he wrote, "They did him the honor of declaring their Knowledge and Approbation of his Services." His commission as acting captain of a captured French merchant ship, the twenty-eight-gun *La Sophie*, was confirmed, and he returned to the North American station.

Mowat would command *La Sophie* for a year. His ship was a participant in Admiral George Rodney's spectacular naval victory over the French in the Battle of the Saintes in the Caribbean, although Henry Mowat earned no special commendation. When the American Revolution ended the next year, *La Sophie* was decommissioned, and Mowat, as was the case with many officers in the military, was put on half-pay. In Mowat's case, his enforced leave was spent mainly in England and lasted until 1795.

Henry Mowat was no longer in command of HMS *Albany* late in 1782 when his former ship was declared "unfit for further military service" and was relegated to patrol duty. The frail vessel was caught in a nasty winter storm on December 28, 1782. It ran on the Northern Triangle ledges in

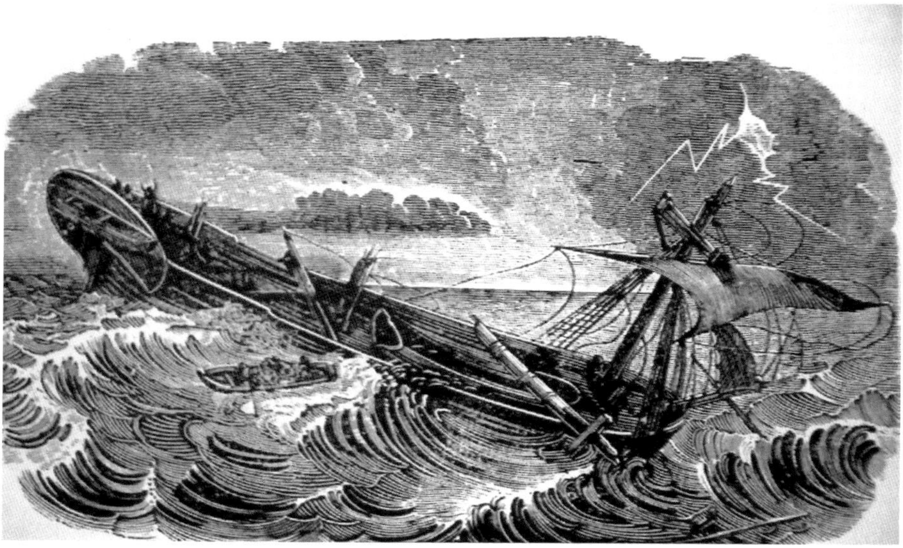

Henry Mowat was no longer in command of *Albany* when it was wrecked in a winter storm in Penobscot Bay in December 1782. *Courtesy of John Flint.*

southern Penobscot Bay with such force that it was quickly apparent that there was no way of getting the vessel off.

Most of the crew managed to get into the ship's two boats—a cutter and a pinnace. The men in the pinnace reached nearby Ash Point, south of Owl's Head. There they chartered a boat owned by a Captain Haskell, which returned to *Albany* and transported the remainder of the crew to Bagaduce.

The cutter got "lost in the vapors" and finally ended up at Markey's Beach on Matinicus Island. By that time, three men had succumbed to the cold. Even today, old timers still call it "Dead Man's Beach." The survivors were carried ashore, defrosted and treated kindly by island inhabitants.

While treating a young British sailor, one of the local women, known as Aunt Susan, noticed tears in his eyes. When she questioned him, he admitted that he had been a member of an *Albany* raiding party that had landed on Matinicus a few months previously and killed her cow for food. Even British sailors could show remorse.

In a bit of irony, Cyrus Eaton writes in his book *History of Thomaston* about a local boy, Joshua Thorndike, who had enlisted shortly after the Battle of Bunker Hill. Thorndike had served aboard a privateer from Falmouth that was captured by HMS *Albany*. He was subsequently kept aboard as a prisoner for nine months.

When he heard about the wreck, the delighted Thorndike and two friends sailed out to the scene and proceeded to salvage as much of value as they could before "the detested craft" went to pieces. The cannons, however, had fallen through the bottom of the boat and remained in the water for the next two hundred years.

Captain John Flint adds a final ironic note. In August 1993, he met the diver who had located the cannon, cannonballs and other items from HMS *Albany* amid the rocks of the Northern Triangles that were lost when the ship sank in 1782. The diver's name was Saltonstall, who was a direct descendent of Dudley Saltonstall, the American commander of the ill-fated Penobscot Expedition.

Chapter 7

Last Years: 1783 to 1798

The treatment of the officer whose case is the subject of the following sheets is perhaps the most extraordinary example of neglect in the annals of the British Navy.

Henry Mowat wrote these bitter words to describe his situation while "on the beach" following his return to London in 1782. His lament was entitled "A relation of the services in which Captain Henry Mowat of the Royal Navy was engaged in America from 1759 to the end of the American War in 1783."

When Mowat returned to England, his life was cloaked in mystery. In addition to his lament, known as a letter of grievance, there are several other

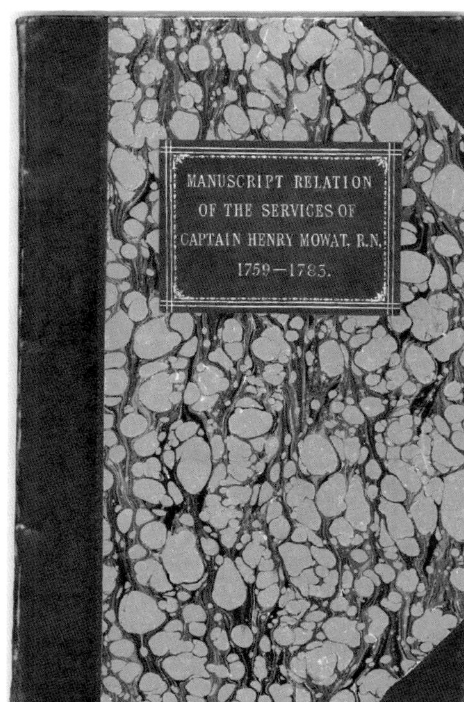

The cover of the letter of grievance that Henry Mowat wrote to King George in 1783 protesting his treatment by the admiralty. *Courtesy of the Maine Historical Society.*

pieces of evidence, however, that provide us with a few clues. These include a letter to the Loyalist Jacob Bailey regarding the care of his son and his will, written shortly before his appointment to command HMS *Assistance*. Beyond that, we can only speculate.

Henry Mowat would live for fifteen, most often frustrating, years after the Revolution until his death in 1798. He appears to have spent most of that time in England, presumably lobbying the admiralty for another command. This finally paid off in 1795, but we are getting ahead of ourselves.

Under British law, a citizen had the right to appeal directly to the king. Known as a letter of grievance, this was the plea of a citizen to right what they considered a grievous offense. Henry Mowat's grievance consisted of a twenty-nine-page letter to King George III in which he reviewed his career as an officer in the Royal Navy.

As a general rule, promotions in the British navy were made on the basis of seniority. What particularly upset Mowat was that during his time of service, junior officers were promoted to post rank (an obsolete term for a captain in the Royal Navy) ahead of him. Not surprisingly, he felt degraded and seriously considered resigning from the navy. His letter is useful as a summary of how Mowat views his career. Selected portions follow.

> *It is the singular instance of an officer who for twenty-eight years has only had a vacancy of eleven months from active service, whose knowledge and experience and attention has attracted the notice of commanders to employ him on important occasions and received the most honorable approbation of his sovereign and ministerial departments with encouraging promises…amidst the daily mortification of seeing every post promotion, except three, put over his head…and now being reduced to the very disagreeable necessity of stating fully his case and to become supplicant for being placed in that proper rank of service which has been all along his due.*

Mowat proceeded to describe his service in the Royal Navy that began in 1759 and continued with his command of the *Canceaux* in the *Atlantic Neptune* survey expedition. His destruction of Falmouth was vaguely referenced in the following sentences: "He was appointed by Admiral Samuel Graves to command the expedition against the seaports to the eastwards of Boston. This done, he cruised in Boston Bay to January 1776." Mowat then reviewed his service throughout the Revolution on "the wretched" (his term) *Albany*, including a detailed description of his heroic actions in the Penobscot Expedition. The final, rather modest, paragraph expressed his hopes for further recognition.

> *Thus ended the attack on Penobscot. It was positively the severest blow received by the American Naval Force during the war...After all was over it was natural to be expected that Sir George Collier would have been supremely happy to have represented this important service in its proper colors and that Captain Mowat would, according to the custom of the service, have been sent home with the account.*

But this was not to be. Mowat recounted how, shortly after the battle, he was ordered to sail up the Penobscot River to reconnoiter the enemy position. Once he was gone, Commodore Collier immediately sent a ship to England carrying an account of the victory that completely ignored Mowat's role.

Mowat concluded his lament to the king by writing:

> *Surely all this must appear to the sovereign, to the board of Admiralty and to all impartial men...a most extraordinary instance of neglect that calls in the loudest manner and without alternative on the justice, honor, interest and spirit of the service and of the state to redress it.*

One can hardly blame Henry Mowat for being distressed. He would spend years in England waiting for a reply from the king while continuing to lobby with the admiralty for a ship. (He finally received his long overdue promotion to post captain late in 1783.) Presumably during this time, he was living in his London house on Milbank Row. Did he return to Nova Scotia where his children were living or did they visit him England? These are unanswered questions.

Jacob Bailey and the Loyalists

In the middle of his lament, Mowat made reference to "Conducting the Loyalists to Nova Scotia." It would have been at this point that he resumed his acquaintance with Jacob Bailey, who had sought refuge in Halifax along with other Loyalists from the Province of Maine.

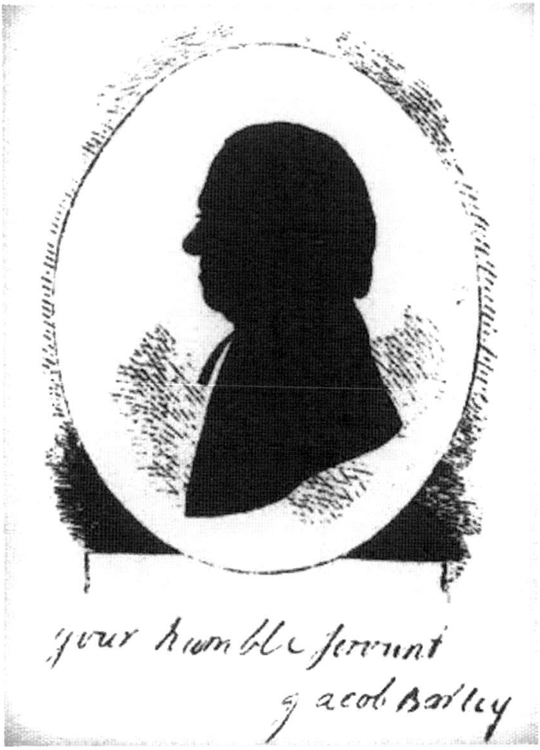

A silhouette of the Loyalist Jacob Bailey with whom Mowat entrusted the education of his son. *Courtesy of the Annapolis Heritage Society Archives.*

Bailey was a Harvard classmate of John Adams and an Anglican minister whom Mowat had met while both men were in Falmouth during Thompson's War. In the process, Mowat had apparently gotten to know the reverend well enough to entrust him with the education of his son.

The Reverend Bailey was one of the few citizens of Falmouth who did not condemn Mowat for his destruction of that town. He described Mowat as "reluctantly, even tearfully carrying out his superior's orders." In his biography of Jacob Bailey, James Leamon writes, "Bailey did not accuse Lieutenant Mowat of 'inhuman barbarity.' Instead Bailey laid blame on Falmouth's Committee of Safety composed of 'tradesmen and men of little property,' aflame with the ideas of liberty." This was hardly a surprising view considering Bailey's Loyalist sympathies.

Jacob Bailey was one of the thousands of Loyalists who were driven from their homes by the radical elements in the American Revolution. Harvard history professor Maya Jasanoff, in her book *Liberty's Exiles*, estimates that about sixty thousand Loyalists left America during the Revolution, taking with them fifteen thousand black slaves. The majority of the Loyalists, about thirty-three thousand, went to Nova Scotia and New Brunswick. In fact, the latter province was created in 1784 to accommodate the influx of refugees.

Another 6,600 expatriates went to Quebec, along with an additional 5,000 who went to Florida and the Caribbean. About 13,000 Loyalists went to Britain, including 5,000 free blacks. Jasanoff's book is a sobering analysis of what she refers to as a "global diaspora."

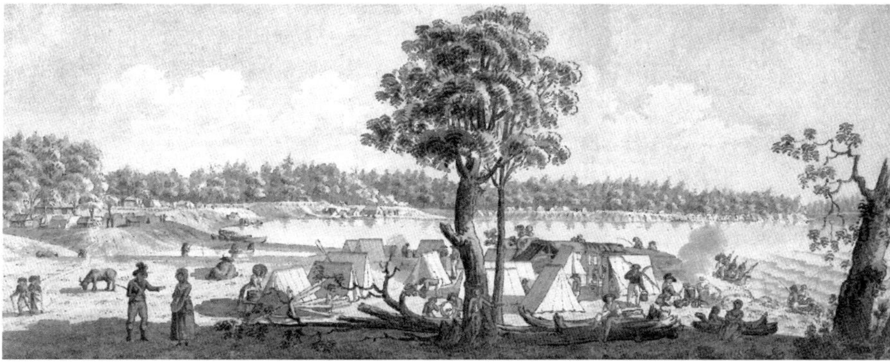

Thousands of American Loyalists fled to Canada after the Revolution. This painting shows a romanticized view of their landing in New Brunswick. *Courtesy of the Library and Archives of Canada*.

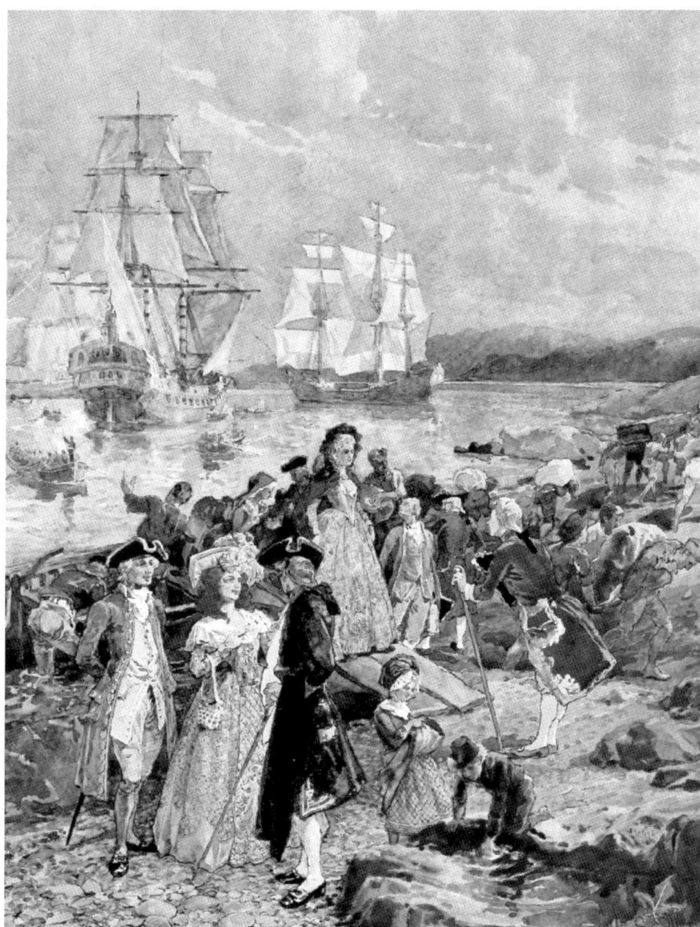

An encampment of Loyalists at Johnstown on the banks of the St. Lawrence River. *Courtesy of the Library and Archives of Canada.*

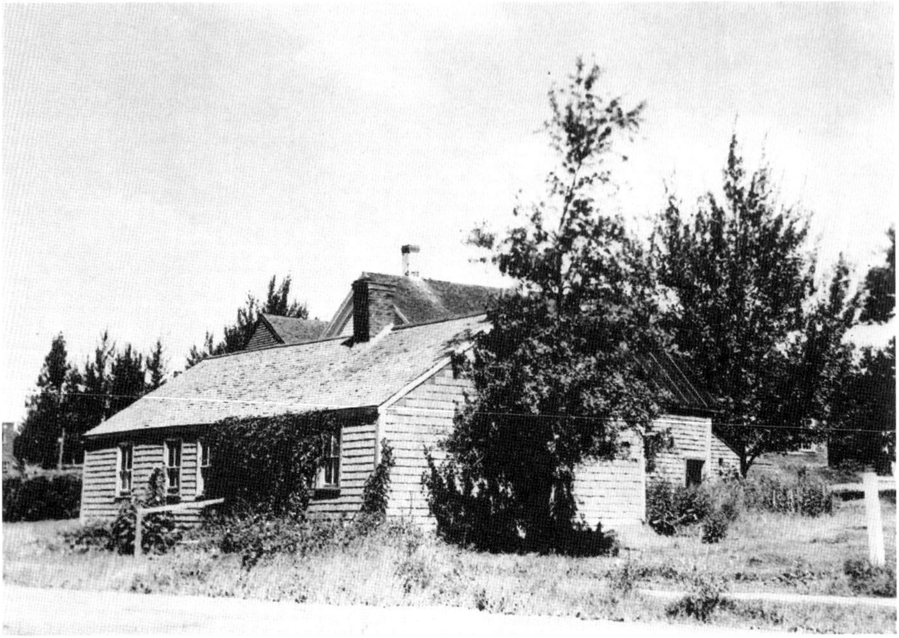

This cabin was moved to Canada in 1783 by a Loyalist family when Castine was returned to Massachusetts after the Revolution. *Courtesy of the Library and Archives of Canada.*

What was the fate of Fort George and the Bagaduce Peninsula that Mowat had fought so hard to keep in British hands? Until the end of the Revolution, the British held the area, which served as a refuge for Loyalists until it was returned to Massachusetts as a part of the peace treaty.

When the British abandoned the fort in 1784, an American representative had not yet arrived to accept the surrender. Some have argued, albeit whimsically, that since Fort George was never legally or politically surrendered to the Americans, it is still technically a British possession. Recently, when the story was related to a group of Scottish tourists at the fort, one inquired, "Well, have you paid your taxes?"

Henry Mowat's Family

What we know about Henry Mowat's immediate family is mostly contained in two documents. The first was a letter he wrote to the Reverend Jacob Bailey in 1782 regarding the care of his son. Excerpts follow.

Rev. Sir, *Halifax the 11th August 1782*

I have for some time been in expectation of receiving your answer to my letter by Mr. Lovett on the subject of my child; but having been given by him and other friends of yours that I may assure myself of your receiving my boy, I have at last determined to send him, and I have made choice of his going by water, as I can not accompany him myself by land, a satisfaction I wished much to have enjoyed...but being now within a few days of leaving for [New?] *York on my way for England, will prevent me the pleasure of seeing you and that of delivering up my dear child into your care, which I now do, with all the endearing and tender feelings of a father, earnestly requesting you to receive him in that light. His aunt accompanies him in the desire of seeing him safe with you, and I shall leave directions with Mr. Thompson (one of his guardians) to pay you the charge of his yearly board and education: Every other necessity will be sent to him by Miss Peak and other friends, whom you will be pleased to correspond with in my absence. I have sent a black servant of my own in order to assist you with the care of him. This man has been mine for the last eight years and I hope he will behave so as to become useful to you as well as to the child, and I have commanded him to obey you the same as myself, and not to do anything or move from your house without your leave. Whatever quarter my professional duty may call me will not prevent my corresponding with you, and I beg you will write often, and put your letters under cover to Alex Thompson, Esquire at Halifax, and he will forward to them to James Sykes Esquire, Crutched Friars, London where they will be taken care of. The indulgence of a very tender mother and other friends over the boy I am fearful may occasion you and Mrs. Bailey more trouble...than I wish it should, but I hope in time his natural disposition will appear, and so far as may be comprehended from his infant years, I am in hopes he will not give more than what may be expected. The wind coming favorable this morning hurries me in hopes of the vessels getting away. My respectful compliments wait on Mrs. Bailey.*

I present the same to you and am, Your most obedient, humble servant,
H. Mowat

Mowat's letter suggests he has been waiting for some time in Halifax for a response from Reverend Bailey before he left for England. A possible

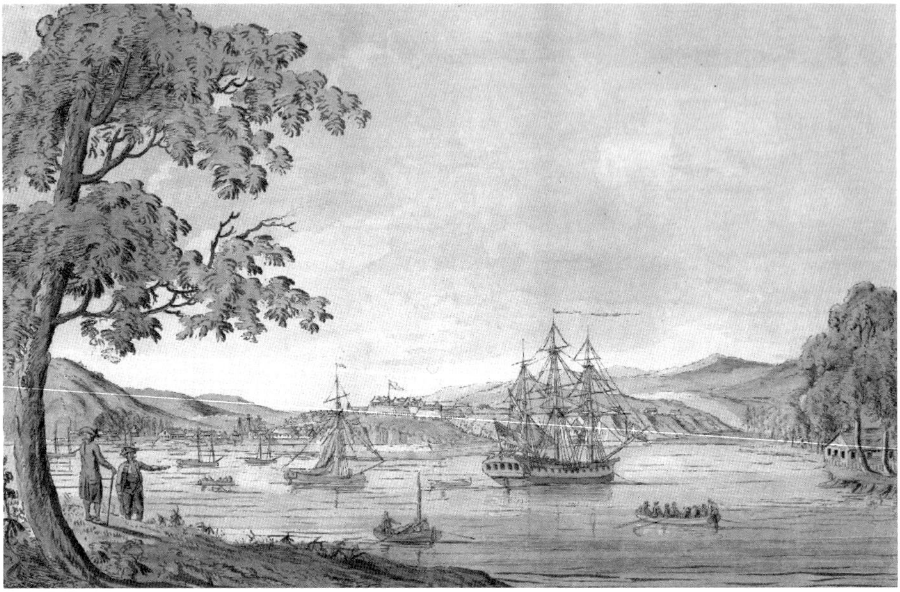

Annapolis Royal, Nova Scotia, is where Mowat left his son to be educated by Jacob Bailey. *Courtesy of the Library and Archives of Canada.*

explanation was that Bailey had moved to Annapolis Royal on the far side of Nova Scotia, a distance of over one hundred miles. It is unclear how long Mowat expected to be away, probably for some time since he left a London address. There is no record of whether he ever returned to visit his son.

The letter raises several interesting questions, most of which we are unable to answer. There is a reference to his son's aunt who will "accompany him" to meet Bailey in Annapolis Royal. Mowat had three brothers but no sisters. As stated in chapter five, no record has been discovered that he was ever married. Might the "aunt" have been a sister of the boy's mother? Or perhaps the term "aunt" simply referred to a close family friend?

We do not know the boy's age or who his mother was, although apparently she was someone with whom Mowat was in contact. Perhaps she was a Loyalist living in Halifax? In the letter, he refers to "The indulgence of a very tender mother and other friends over the boy." This suggests that Mowat was worried that the child's mother and her friends would spoil the boy. In the letter, Mowat tries to reassure Bailey, as well as himself, that his son's "natural disposition" was sufficiently strong to resist such temptations.

Mowat, however, appears reluctant to remove his son from the environs of Nova Scotia. Was this in response to pressure from the child's mother? Finally, there is the reference to Mowat's slave of eight years who did not accompany him to England but instead was left with Reverend Bailey to help care for the boy.

The second document regarding Mowat's family is his will, written in 1795 and probated after his death in 1799. As noted, Henry Mowat had finally received his long-sought post captain's commission in 1782 or 1783. He was given command of a ship and ordered to the Caribbean in 1795.

Mowat's will is also a revealing document. He gives his address as Milbank Row, evidence that he was still living in London. It is logical to assume that at the age of sixty-one, Captain Mowat felt he needed to put his affairs in order before departing from England for possibly the last time.

> *This is the Last Will and testament of me, Henry Mowat of Milbank Row, Westminster in the County of Middlesex, a Captain in the Royal Navy of Great Britain being of Sound and disposing mind memory and understanding.*
>
> *First I direct that all my just Debts, funeral Expenses and Legacies shall be paid by my Executors here after named.*
>
> *I give and bequeath to my well deserving friend Mrs. Easter* [sic] *Moore at this time in the charge of my house and family all such plate and household furniture as may be in the said house or belonging to me at the time of my Death.*
>
> *I also bequeath to the said Mrs. Moore the fourth part of all the Interest arising from the Dividends or other property at my decease.*
>
> *I give and bequeath to my daughter Mary Ann Mowat the Interest arising from the same after payment of the Interest mentioned to Mrs. Moore to be applied of the use and to the furnishing of the Education of her the said Mary Ann Mowat until she shall attain her Age of twenty one years of age or the day of Marriage, which shall happen first.*
>
> *The other half of all the money now in the funds, or may be at the time of my death, and of all the other property herein mentioned, I give and bequeath to my son William Mowat the interest arising from the same is to be applied to his use and the finishing of his education and his attaining his age of twenty one years the said half share of all the property mentioned in this will.*
>
> *I leave my gold watch, seals and swords to my son William and at the death of Mrs. Moore all such plate and household furniture as may be left by her is to be at the disposal of the said Mary Ann.*

> *I do here by nominate and appoint James Sykes Esquire of Arundel street and on his death his son James, Robert Marsh of Sloan Square, Charles Smith of James Street, as Executioners of this my Will and Guardians of my said two children.*
>
> *And lastly I do hereby revoke all former and other Will or Wills by me at any time and declare this to be my Last Will and Testament.*

Although the will states that Mowat's son was named William, other sources refer to him as John Alexander. For this, we have no explanation.

In addition to his will, there is only one other brief reference to Mowat's daughter, Mary Ann. This appears in *Frontier Missionary*, a biography of Jacob Bailey written by William Bartlet in 1853. Bailey and his wife had just arrived in Halifax, Nova Scotia, in June 1779 when the minister related the following event. "We had breakfast with an old lady and a very pretty, genteel young Miss, about twelve, the natural daughter of the famous Captain Mowat."

FINAL COMMAND

The fifty-gun frigate *Assistance* was Post-Captain Mowat's first ship since 1783. It was unusual for a senior officer to be brought out of virtual retirement and returned to active duty. The probable explanation was that England was involved in a bitter struggle with Revolutionary France and that the admiralty was doing everything it could to strengthen British sea power around the world.

Is also is likely that England wanted to provide support for the beleaguered United States against France in the so-called Quasi-War, an undeclared maritime war between those two countries. Although they were fighting the same enemy, the Royal Navy and the United States Navy did not share operational plans or discuss the deployment of their forces. The British did, however, sell the American government naval stores and munitions. In addition, the two navies shared a system of signals by which each could recognize the other's warships at sea.

Mowat was named second in command of the American Squadron deployed against the French in the Caribbean. We know his ship was involved in at least one engagement when *Assistance* captured a French frigate in 1796. Two years later, *Assistance* was cruising a few miles off of the entrance to

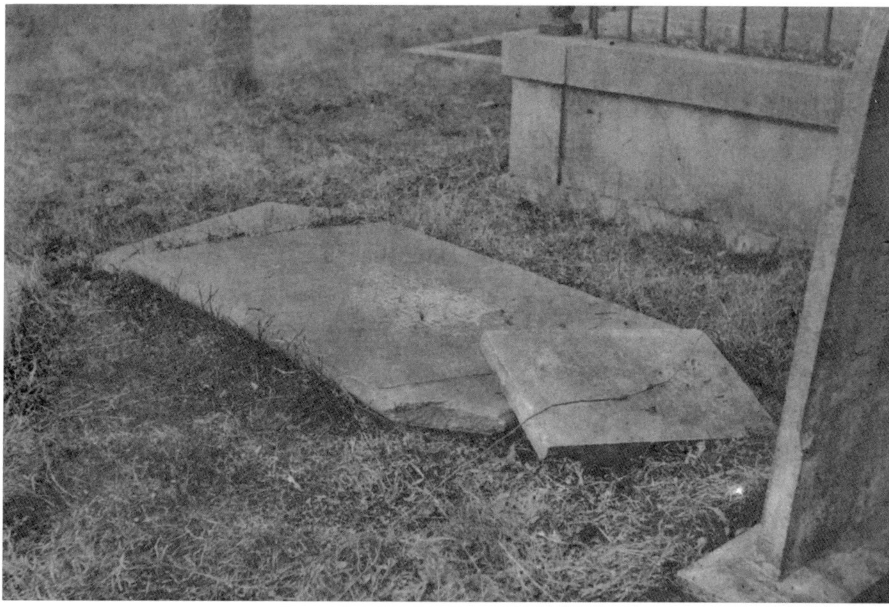

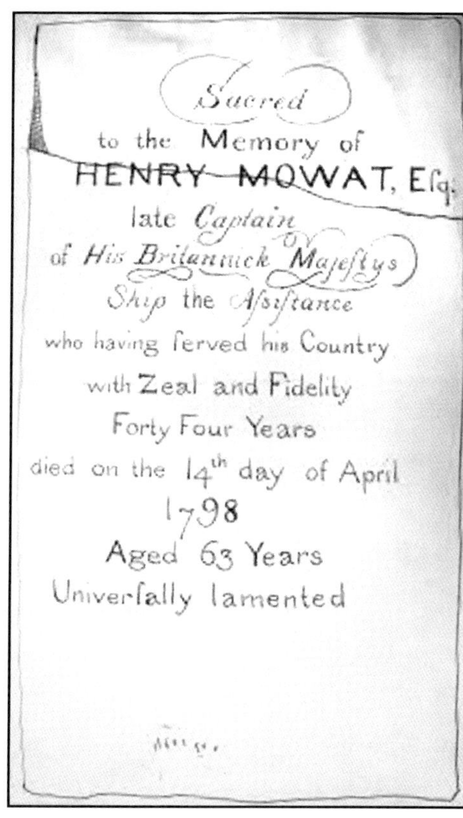

Above: Henry Mowat was buried in Hampton, Virginia, where his body was taken after his death at sea. *Courtesy of the Maine Historical Society.*

Right: A sketch of the inscription on Mowat's gravestone. *Courtesy of the Maine Historical Society.*

Chesapeake Bay when Captain Mowat was stricken by a fatal stroke in his cabin. He died aboard his ship on April 14, 1798.

His body was taken ashore, and he was buried in the graveyard of St. John's Episcopal Church in Hampton, Virginia, where his gravestone can be seen today. It seems likely that the officers of *Assistance* erected the memorial, since he would have been unknown to the citizens of Hampton.

Would Henry Mowat have attained the rank of admiral? There is an unsubstantiated family story that the elderly captain was about to return to England for the coveted promotion, but of course, he never made it.

Appendix

Henry Mowat's Service Record in the Royal Navy

Ship	Rank	Dates
Antelope (54)*	able seaman	1755 (5 months, after merchant service of 3 years)
Chesterfield (44)	Mid/Master's Mate	1755–57 (2 years, 1 month)
Ramilles (82)	Midshipman	1757 (5 months)
Baltimore (8)	Lieutenant	1759
Aldborough (24)	Lieutenant	1760
Canceaux (8)	Lieutenant in command	1764–76
Milford (28)	Lieutenant acting in command	1777
Scarborough (22)	Lieutenant acting in command	1777
Albany (16)	Lieutenant in command	1777–82
Sophie (28)	Acting Captain	1782–83 (On Half Pay) September 1783 to May 1795
Assistance (50)	Captain	1795–98

*Number of guns

Bibliography

Secondary Sources

Allen, Gardner, W. *Massachusetts Privateers of the Revolution*. Boston, MA: Massachusetts Historical Society, 1927.

———. *A Naval History of the American Revolution*. Vols. 1 and 2. Boston, MA: Houghton Mifflin Company, 1913.

Avery, Elroy M. *A History of the United States and Its People*. Reprint, Cleveland, OH: Burrows Brothers Company, 1908.

Bartlet, William S. *The Frontier Missionary*. New York: Stanford and Swords, 1853.

Buck, Rufus. *A History of the Town of Bucksport*. N.p. 1857.

Buker, George E. *The Penobscot Expedition: Commodore Saltonstall and the Massachusetts Conspiracy of 1779*. Annapolis, MD: Naval Institute Press, 2002.

Conforti, Joseph A. *Creating Portland*. Durham: University of New Hampshire Press, 2007.

Daughan, George C. *If By Sea: The Forging of the American Navy*. New York: Basic Books, 2008.

Duncan, Roger F. *Coastal Maine: A Maritime History*. Woodstock, VT: Countryman Press, 1992.

Fischer, David Hackett. *Paul Revere's Ride*. New York: Oxford University Press, 1994.

Flood, Charles Bracelen. *Rise and Fight Again*. New York: Dodd, Mead and Company, 1976.

Gratwick, Harry. *Hidden History of Maine*. Charleston, SC: The History Press, 2010.

History of Penobscot County Maine, With Illustrations and Biographical Sketches. Cleveland, OH: Williams, Chase & Company, 1882.

Hornsby, Stephen J. *Surveyors of Empire*. Montreal, Canada: McGill-Queen's University Press, 2011.

Hutchinson, Vernal. *When the Revolution Came*. Ellsworth, ME: Ellsworth American, 1972.

Islesboro Historical Society. *History of Islesboro, 1893–1984*. Portland, ME: Islesboro Historical Society, 1984.

Jack, D.R. *The Mowat Family in Acadiensis*. vol. 8. Canada, 1908.

Jasanoff, Maya. *Liberty's Exiles: American Loyalists in the Revolutionary World*. New York: Alfred A. Knopf, 2011.

Leamon, James S. *The Reverend Jacob Bailey: Maine Loyalist*. Amherst: University of Massachusetts Press, 2012.

———. *Revolution Downeast*. Amherst: University of Massachusetts Press, 1993.

Philbrick, Nathaniel. *Bunker Hill*. New York: Penguin Books, 2013.

Preston, Antony. *Navies of the American Revolution*. Englewood Cliffs, NJ: Prentice-Hall, 1975.

Shaw, Henry I. *The Penobscot Expedition*. Bicentennial Lecture Series. Bangor, ME: Bangor Historical Society, 1976.

Stover, Arthur Douglas. *Eminent Mainers*. Gardiner, ME: Tilbury House, 2006.

Tilley, John A. *The British Navy and the American Revolution*. Columbia: University of South Carolina Press, 1987.

Trevelyan, Sir George Otto. *The American Revolution*. vol. 3. New York: Longmans, Green and Company, 1922.

Varney, George J. *History of Waldo County, Maine*. Boston, MA: B.B. Russell, 1886.

Wheeler, George Augustus and Henry Warren. *A History of Brunswick, Topsham and Harpswell, Maine*. Heritage Classic. 1878.

Williamson, Joseph. *The British Occupation of Penobscot During the Revolution*. Read before the Maine Historical Society, December 21, 1883.

Woodard, Colin. *The Lobster Coast*. New York: Viking, 2004.

Bibliography

Primary Sources

Bangor (ME) Whig and Courier, August 13, 1846.

Banks, Charles Edward. Scrapbook Containing Biographical Materials of Captain Henry Mowat, R.N. 1735–98. Maine Historical Society, Portland.

———. Scrapbook Containing Materials Pertaining to Captain Mowat's Destruction of Falmouth, October 18, 17751. Maine Historical Society, Portland.

———. Scrapbook of Thompson's War in Falmouth, 1775. Maine Historical Society, Portland.

Baxter, James P. *Documentary History of the State of Maine*. vol. 17. Portland, ME, 1913.

Calef, John. *The Journal of the Siege of Penobscot*. New York, 1910.

Deposition of Reverend Wiswell.

History of Penobscot County. Cleveland, OH: Williams, Chase and Company, 1882.

Journal of Lt. John Gwatkin, RN, of HMS Albany. Penobscot Marine Museum, Searsport, ME.

Mowat, Henry. "Captain Henry Mowat's Account." *Magazine of History* 3 (1910): 333–43.

Mowat, Henry. *Voyage of the* Canceaux, *1764–1776*. Annotated by Andrew J. Wahll. Bowie, MD: Heritage Books, 2003.

Archival Materials Consulted at the Following Locations:

Castine Historical Society, Castine, ME.

Deer Isle and Stonington Historical Society, Deer Isle, ME.

Fogler Library. Special Collections Department. University of Maine, Orono, ME.

Islesboro Historical Society, Islesboro, ME.

Library and Archives of Canada. References Services Division, Ottawa.

Maine Historical Society, Portland.

Penobscot Marine Museum, Searsport, ME.

Public Archives of Nova Scotia, Halifax.

Thomaston Historical Society, Thomaston, ME.

Vinalhaven Historical Society, Vinalhaven, ME.

Index

A

B

Index

Index

About the Author

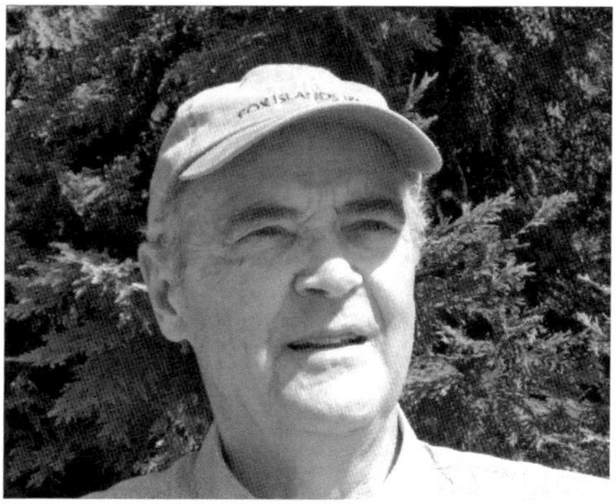

Courtesy of Myles McDonald.

Harry Gratwick is a seasonal resident of Vinalhaven Island in Penobscot Bay. A retired teacher, Gratwick had a forty-five-year career as a secondary school educator. He spent most of those years at Germantown Friends School in Philadelphia, Pennsylvania, where he chaired the history department and coached the baseball team.

Gratwick is an active member of the Vinalhaven Historical Society and has written extensively on maritime history for two Island Institute publications, *The Working Waterfront* and *Island Journal*.

Gratwick is a graduate of Williams College and has a master's degree from Columbia University. Harry and his wife, Tita, have two sons, a Russian daughter-in-law and two grandsons.

Visit him at www.harrygratwick.com.

Also by Harry Gratwick:

Penobscot Bay: People, Ports and Pastimes
Hidden History of Maine
Mainers in the Civil War
Stories from the Maine Coast
The Forts of Maine
Historic Shipwrecks of Penobscot Bay